AMAZON ECHO SHOW 5 COMPLETE GUIDE

The Ultimate Guide to Master Your Amazon Echo Show 5 and Amazon Echo Dot with Alexa

Scott Brown

CONTENTS

Introduction

Amazon's Echo family just keeps on growing. If you've got a gap somewhere in your house, there's almost certainly an Alexa-infused gadget you can fill it with.

If Amazon let me design my dream smart speaker, it wouldn't be all that different from the Echo Show 5. It's small enough to fit on my desk, but its screen is large enough to see from across the room. It has a physical switch to cover the camera lens for privacy. And it's just as useful as a "dumb" device as it is a smart one.

The Echo Show 5 strikes a perfect balance between seen and unseen. If the original conceit of the Echo speaker was that it would blend into your home and only make itself known when called upon, the Echo Show flipped that notion with a giant body and a 7-inch display that made it more of a centerpiece than an accessory. You'll want to display the Show 5 somewhere visible, too; but it won't overtake the room it's in. If anything, it will complement it, like a vase or a piece of art.

That said, there are two main rooms that are natural fits for the Echo Show 5: a bedroom or a home office. At 5.8 x 3.4 inches, it's definitely larger than the 4.5 x 2.9-inch Lenovo Smart Clock and the circular Echo Spot, but not in a clumsy way. My test unit has been on my desk since I got it, and it feels right at home without dominating my workspace or stealing my focus.

The Echo Show 5's design follows the path forged by Amazon's other smart displays, with a triangular, white-on-black base that props it at a slight angle. Its rectangular display is at once familiar and practical, tacitly admitting that the circular Echo Spot isn't ideal. On that note, I assume the Echo Show 5 will show the Echo Spot the door, but the latter's quirky and adorable form will always have a place in my home.

The Echo Show 5 improves on more than just the shape of the Echo Spot. While the Show 5 also has a down-firing speaker—which is something of a waste of its fabric-wrapped body—the 4W, 1.65-inch speaker sounds much fuller and bossier than the Echo Spot's . You're won't buy either of these devices for audiophile-quality sound, but I came away impressed with the Echo Show 5. Throw in a 3.5mm analog audio output, Amazon Music lyrics, and native support for every major streaming service, and you have a damn near perfect smart speaker for music lovers.

The speaker grill is beneath the Echo Show 5, which muffles the sound a bit. But even if you don't listen to playlists all day, the Echo Show 5 is still a great companion. On a nightstand, it's just as good a bedside alarm clock as the Lenovo Smart Clock—including the ambient sunrise lighting feature that gradually brightens the screen, and the ability to tap the top of the frame to snooze an alarm—and on a kitchen counter, it'll be a great recipe book and measurement converter. I wouldn't be opposed to smaller bezels and rounded corners on the display, but as it stands, the Echo Show 5 is a remarkable evolution from the cylindrical original. Here is a complete guide to master your Echo Sh

Getting started with the Amazon Echo Show

Setting up the Echo Show is not complicated and the set up is not that different from other devices in the Echo family. It normally takes me about five minutes to finish the set up. Before you set up the Echo Show, there are certain things that must be in place:

- The Echo Show unit.

- A smartphone/tablet (or a computer).

- An active internet connection (and router with WIFI capabilities).

- Your Amazon Prime Account details

Note: Don't fret if you don't have access to a smartphone or computer, the device screen can also be used to do the set up. Follow these steps to set up your Echo Show:

- Download the Alexa App to your PC/Mac or Smartphone Tablet. The app can be downloaded from the Amazon Appstore, Apple

App Store, or Google Play. You can also download the app directly from Alexa.amazon.com using Safari, Chrome, Firefox, Microsoft Edge, or Internet Explorer 10 or higher.

- After downloading the Alexa App, find a spot for your Echo Show (should be eight inches or more from any walls or windows) and plug it into an AC power outlet using the power adapter. It will turn on automatically.

- Once on, you should hear Alexa say, "Hello, your Echo Device is ready for setup."

- Next, there are onscreen prompts for Select Language, Connect to Wi-Fi (have your password/wireless key code), Confirm Time Zone, Log in to your Amazon account (should be the same as the account you have on your smartphone), and then read and accept the Echo Show Terms and Conditions notice.

- If there are any available firmware updates, the screen will display an updates ready message.

Tap Install Now, shown on the screen. Installation may take several minutes. Wait until the screen notifies you that installation of the update(s) is complete.

After the updates are installed, an Introducing Echo Show video will become available that will familiarize you with some of its features. After viewing the video (recommended), Alexa will say, "Your Echo Show is ready."

Using Alexa Voice Recognition and Touchscreen

To start using the Echo Show, say "Alexa" and then state a command or ask a question. Once Alexa responds, you are ready to go. Alexa is the default Wake Word. However, you can also change your wake word:

- Command Alexa to Go to settings or use the touch screen to get to the Settings menu.
- Once there, select Device Options, and select Wake Word.

- Your additional Wake Word choices are Echo, Amazon, and Computer. If you like one, select it and then tap Save.

Pairing Mobile Devices with Echo Show

The Echo show is Bluetooth-enabled which can be used as a standalone Bluetooth speaker or to stream audio services from your tablet or phone. This is expedient for persons who use Google Play Music and iTunes on their mobiles. Follow these instructions to pair mobile devices with Echo Show.

- Go to your mobile device settings and put on the Bluetooth

- Go to the Settings of your Alexa and tap Bluetooth and pairing will occur or say to Alexa "Pair my phone." And Alexa will replied, "Connected to---phone."

- You will see the Bluetooth settings on the screen with a list of Bluetooth devices paired and whether there is a connection.

- Your phone or other device's Bluetooth Settings

will list your Alexa once they are paired.

- If you want to exit the Bluetooth mode before the connection, tell Alexa "Cancel," to stop Bluetooth pairing.

- **Note**: Echo Show can only pair with one device at a time. If Echo Show has been paired with multiple devices, it will only connect to the most recent one. You can disconnect a paired device by saying to Alexa, "Disconnect."

How To Set Up The Amazon Echo Dot

Setting up the Echo Dot only takes a few minutes, even if you're new to smart home devices. Here's how to get your Amazon Echo Dot up and running.

1. Download and open the Alexa app (Android and iOS) on your smartphone or tablet.

2. Select Devices in the lower right corner.

3. Press the Plus sign in the top right corner, or press the hamburger menu (the three horizontal lines) in the upper left corner

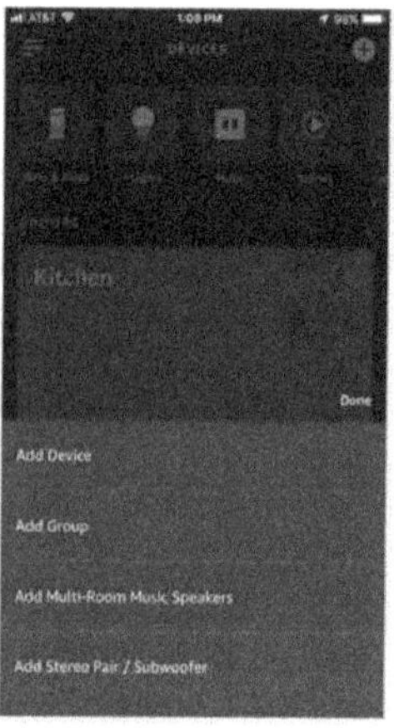

4. Select "Add Device."

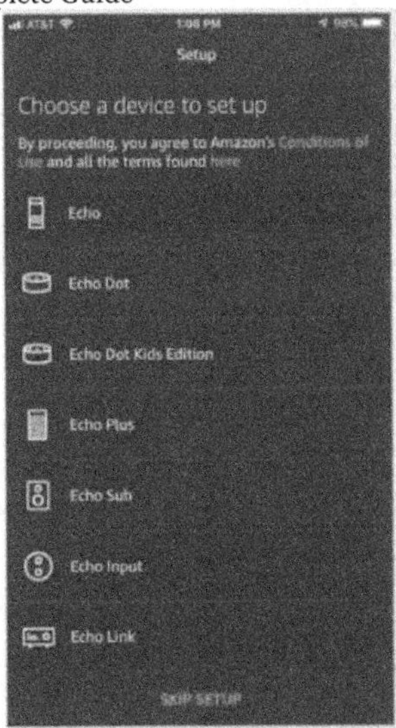

5. Press the Amazon Echo icon, followed by the Echo Dot icon that appears on the next screen. Then, press the image of the third-generation Echo Dot.

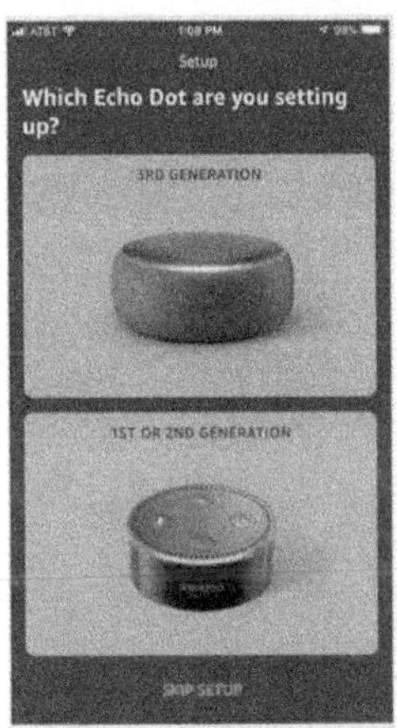

6. Plug in your Echo Dot using the included power adapter. Once the blue light ring has turned orange, your device is in Setup Mode.

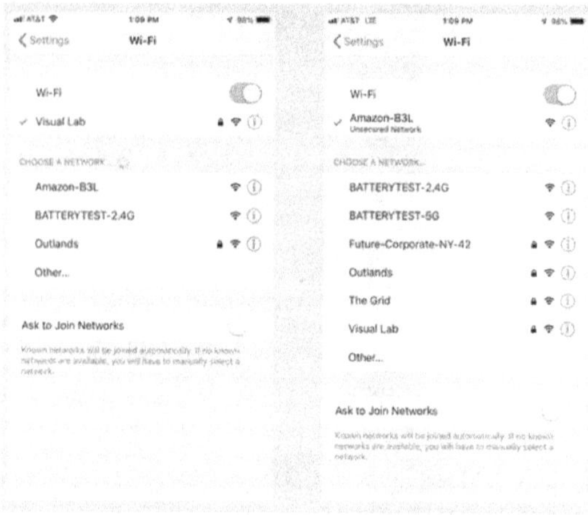

7. Wait for your Echo Dot to appear on your phone and select it. You'll be prompted to go to your Wi-Fi settings. Once there, select the network called "Amazon-XXX." Then, return to the Alexa app.

8. Choose the Wi-Fi network to which you want to connect your Echo Dot. Enter your password if required.

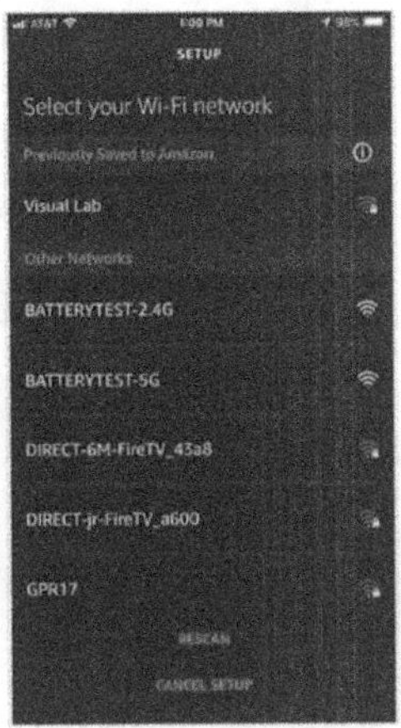

9. Select the external speaker your Echo Dot will be using. If you won't be connecting this device to an external speaker, skip this step.

10. Select the room where your Echo Dot is located (or create a new room).

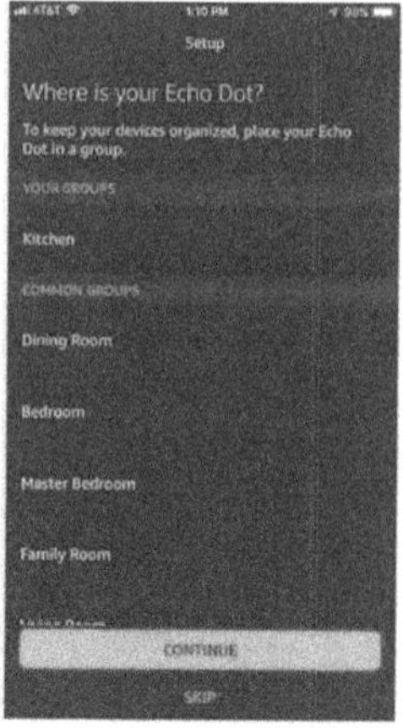

Congratulations: You've set up your Echo Dot!

How to Make Amazon Echo Understand Your Voice

The Amazon Echo smart speaker is totally reliant on understanding your voice. But that doesn't mean it will understand every accent of vocal tick right out of the box. That's why Amazon built in some tricks to make it better learn your vocal inflections.

1. Open the Alexa app on your smartphone.

2. Tap the three bar menu button on the top left.

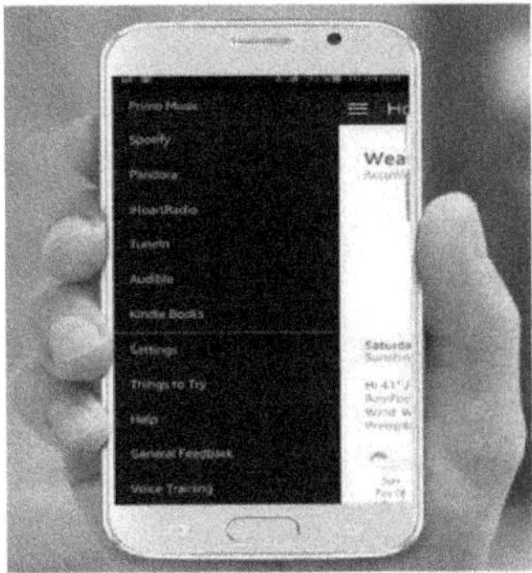

3. Scroll down and tap Voice Training.

4. Tap Start Session.

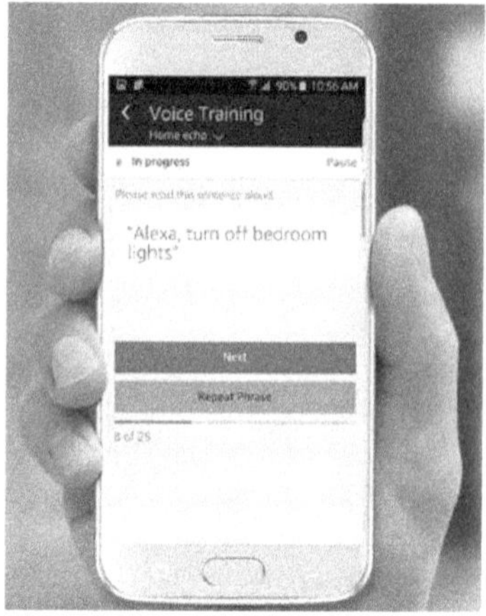

5. Get close to the Amazon Echo and say each of the 25 phrases that appear on the screen. After each tap Next.

6. Tap Start a New Session if you want Alexa to keep learning, or simply go to the home page.

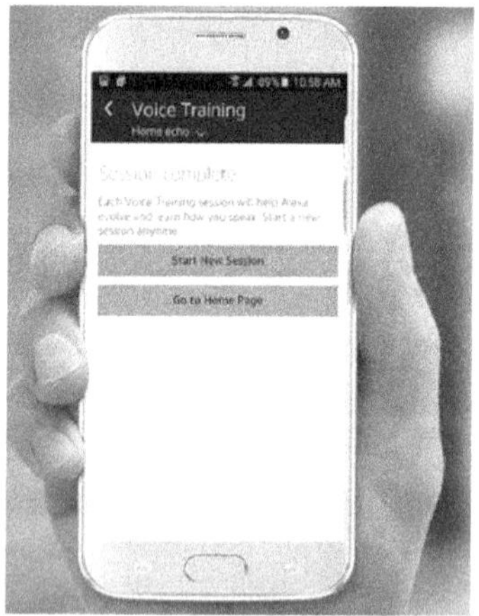

You can repeat this process if you notice a pattern of Alexa misunderstanding your commands. You can also see what Alexa heard in the app. If it's incorrect, tap No. This will continue you her education.

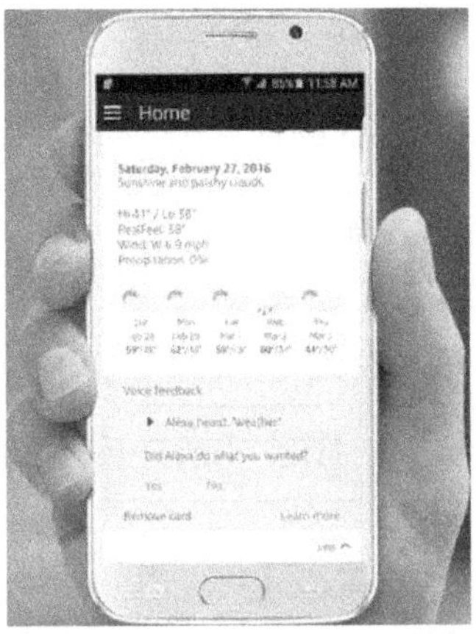

How to Set Up The Alexa Voice Remote

As mentioned previously, this feature is optional but it is very essential mostly when there is noise in the space that will cause you to shout or put Alexa into confusion, the remote becomes a good alternative to speaking across to Alexa. You can shop for the Alexa remote on Amazon, but be careful not to purchase Alexa voice remote for Amazon Fire TV and Fire TV stick.

I love exploring the capabilities of my Echo Show. You can speak to Alexa, "Shop for Alexa voice remote," and look the display on the screen. If you have activated 1-click in your Amazon account and you click **buy this** on the Alexa screen, an instant purchase will be made except you say, "Cancel the order" to reverse the purchase.

Normally, the Alexa remote pair automatically with the device once the batteries are installed, but if doesn't happen, you can pair it through the Echo Show device or via Alexa App. To pair the remote using the App, go to **Settings**; select your device (your Echo Show), then select **pair remote**. Simple! You can also pair the remote using the device by swiping down from the top of the touchscreen, tap **settings**, then scroll down a little and tap **device options,** on the device option page, choose **pair Amazon Echo Remote** and follow the brief guideline.

What Is Alexa Voice Shopping, and How Do You Use It?

Although voice shopping is still a nascent retail channel, studies show it's set to take off. As we approach Amazon Prime Day, more people than ever may be curious about the voice-assisted medium.

A recent survey by Sumo Heavy indicates that only 1 in 5 consumers has tried voice shopping. However, data suggests voice shopping will increase as digital assistants like Alexa and Google Assistant make their want into more homes. In fact, the industry expected to jump from the $2 billion industry it is today to $40 billion by 2022. Moreover, Amazon is expected to dominate the new channel with the largest market share of smart speakers, currently more than twice that of its competitors Google and Microsoft.

Amazon's Alexa Voice Shopping service lets you make purchases or get a rundown of the day's best deals with the sound of your voice. For instance, if you decide you need some paper towels, you can shout out your request to Alexa, and within days, your order will arrive at your doorstep.

The e-tailer has even offered exclusive Alexa-only discounts to consumers who purchase or re-order items via an Alexa device.

But there are some requirements you should know about. First, you'll have to be an Amazon customer, and you'll want to be a Prime member subscriber to make Alexa Voice Shopping much easier. You'll also need a device with Alexa built in, such as an Echo Dot.

If you can tick all those boxes, Alexa Voice Shopping might be a great alternative to brick-and-mortar stores and, yes, traditional online shopping.

What is Alexa Voice Shopping?

Alexa Voice Shopping is a service from Amazon that allows you to place orders through the online retail giant with just a voice command.

So, if you have an Alexa-enabled product, like an Amazon Echo or even the Amazon app for Android and iOS, all you have to do is tell Alexa what you want to buy. Alexa immediately searches Amazon to find the product and confirms it has picked the item you want. If you respond with a "yes," the order is placed.

On its Alexa Voice Shopping page, Amazon says you can choose from the millions of products it offers, and to help you save a few bucks, you can even ask Alexa what deals there might be on certain products.

Still not exactly sure how it might work? Here's a scenario:

Let's just say you've been parched all day, and you're drinking bottle after bottle of Fiji water. Suddenly, you realize you're all out. Rather than drive to the store in the scorching summer heat, you decide to order a case through Amazon and have it delivered to your house.

So, you say, "Alexa, order Fiji Natural Artesian Water." Alexa will hear that and will respond by telling you that it's found an option on Amazon for a certain price. Then, Alexa will ask you if it's OK to order. If you're happy with the product Alexa found, you can say "yes," and your order will be placed.

Now, sit back, relax and wait for your water to arrive.

Where can I find Alexa Voice Shopping?

One of the nice things about Amazon Alexa is that it's ubiquitous. The virtual personal assistant runs on a host of devices, allowing you to interact with it to search the web, place online orders and keep track of your schedule.

Here's a list of devices that are compatible with Alexa Voice Shopping:

- Amazon Echo
- Amazon Tap
- Amazon Echo Dot
- Amazon Fire TV
- Amazon Fire Tablets
- Amazon app (available on iOS and Android)

Can I ask Alexa sophisticated questions?

Yes, Alexa Voice Shopping can understand sophisticated queries. So, for example, you can ask for specific brands of household goods.

Say you have a particular coffee brand you like. You can order it through Alexa Voice Shopping by saying, "Alexa, order Newman's Own K-Cups." Alexa will find it on Amazon and facilitate the purchase.

Don't go easy on Alexa — the virtual assistant can handle it.

Do I need to be a Prime member?

Technically, Alexa Voice Shopping is available to anyone who uses the aforementioned Amazon hardware or software. However, if you're a Prime member, Alexa Voice Shopping is far more useful.

If you want to place orders through one of Amazon's devices, you must be a Prime member who has 1-Click ordering enabled. If you're not a Prime member and do not have 1-Click ordering turned on, you won't be able to access Alexa Voice Shopping from one of Amazon's many devices.

If you plan to try out the voice service through the Amazon app, however, all that changes.

From the Amazon app, you can search for and add an item to your cart with voice commands issued through Alexa Voice Shopping. Better yet, you don't need to be a Prime member or have 1-Click ordering turned on to do it.

If you want to buy whatever you put into your cart, though, you need to head back to your app and manually place your order.

What is Amazon's Choice?

When you haven't bought certain items before and you're simply looking for recommendations within the product category, Alexa Voice Shopping will return results from the company's Amazon's Choice line of products.

Amazon's Choice is a curated collection of products, across a wide array of categories, that have high ratings and solid prices. Think of the Amazon's

Choice collection as Amazon's picks for the best products in its store.

While Alexa Voice Shopping will allow you to pick the product, Amazon's Choice gives you quick access to some of the best products on the service.

How do I set up a confirmation code?

Although it's nice to be able to quickly add a product to your cart and buy it, that won't be helpful if you don't want to make a purchase right away.

To address those situations, Amazon allows you to set up a confirmation code with Alexa. So, after you ask to add something to the cart, Alexa won't actually charge your card and process the transaction until you provide your four-digit code.

To set up the confirmation code, you need to launch the Alexa app and go to Menu > Settings. From there, you can choose Voice Purchasing and set a four-digit code.

Once that code is saved, when you place an order, Alexa will ask if you'd like to proceed with the purchase by providing your four-digit code. If you ignore Alexa, your order will remain in the queue and will not process until you're ready.

When you are ready to buy, simply tell Alexa your code.

OK, I goofed. Can I cancel a purchase?

If you made an accidental purchase, all is not lost. But you'd better move quickly.

If you ordered through Amazon's 1-Click, you have 30 minutes to cancel it before it's completed.

To cancel an order within the allotted time frame, go to your Amazon account, and click on Your Orders. There, you'll see a list of orders and the option, if applicable, to Cancel Items. Next, you can check the box next to each item you want to cancel. When you're done, click "Cancel checked items."

Your order is now canceled.

Can I order more than one item with Alexa Voice Shopping?

Well, yes and no.

If you're hoping to buy two different items in the same order, you won't be able to do so with Alexa Voice Shopping. Instead, each request for products will be its own order. So, if you want to buy a new phone charger, shampoo, water and chips, all four items will be listed in separate orders.

However, if you want to buy more than one of a certain item, you can. So if you want two bags of chips, you can request your quantity, and Alexa will take care of the rest.

You can also create a shopping list to make multiple purchases easier. To create a shopping list, go to the menu in the top left corner of the Alexa app and select Lists, then Create List. You can also collaborate with family and roommates to make sure you get everything your household needs. To invite someone, select the list you want to collaborate on, and click on the "+Invite" button. Alexa will provide a link which you can send to others, or it can send an email to them automatically.

How to set up and use Alexa Routines for a smarter home

Alexa Routines gives you seamless, single command control of your home, in other words the kind of features you actually want from a smart home.

Rather than simply turn on and off devices, which has long been a feature of Groups within the Alexa app, Routines is more about how those devices act on your command. That means dimming some lights, changing the color of others, or perhaps firing up your heating to a certain temperature. Amazon also added new abilities back in April when it added music, podcasts and radio to the mix.

Obvious ideas for Routines are "movie time" and "bed time," the latter of which could have genuine benefits for a good night's sleep. Getting your bed time lighting and temperature set can aid a more restful sleep, which makes Alexa Routines not just fun, but great for your health. Here's how to start your Routines in Alexa.

It's simple to start an Alexa Routine: just head to the Alexa app (see above), go to the menu and choose Routines. A list of your current Routines will be listed, and Amazon will recommend a couple under Featured, just to get you started. Either tap one of these, or just hit the + in the top-right to start one from scratch.

When this happens is essentially the short command you're going to give Alexa. Press the + to add one and you can choose between a number of options. There's vocal Alexa commands, timed Routines, device-based Routines, geolocation-based routines and Echo Button-based Routines.

If you chose a command, you just have to type it in manually. Whatever you want to say, keep it natural. Device-based Routines will use your new Echo Plus' temperature sensor. So when the temperature is above or below a certain temperature, you can activate certain things - like a smart plug connected to your fan when it's too hot.

Geolocation will use your phone's location to trigger events when you arrive or leave certain locations, including your home and work. This is pretty huge because you can have certain actions trigger when you arrive some place. For instance, you can activate your lights when you come home. Or maybe Alexa reads off your calendar when you get to work.

Once you've selected how to trigger your Routine, it's time to build it up. To do that just press the + next to Add action.

Alexa smart home actions

Once you have selected the conditions for your routine, it's then time to add all the actions. To do this just tap the + icon next to Add action. The actions you add to your Routine are the elements that will be controlled when you say your chosen command. We're going to go through the possibilities quickly below, but it's worth noting that you don't have to build these up from scratch. If you have specific Groups or Scenes set up in the Alexa app, you can shortcut to run these.

"Alexa, Bedtime" for example could be turning off the existing downstairs lights group, and then turning on the lights in your bedroom, but to 50% brightness. If you're wanting to build this up device by device, this is what you can do:

Lights

Smart lights can be added to your Routine – and it's not just on/off control. You can set the brightness, hue, tone and color of compatible smart bulbs.

Thermostats

At present you can control heating zones within your home, but this is simply an on/off setting, which will refer to the default temperature in Smart Home listing. It's not possible to select bespoke temperatures for the Routine, for example.

Plugs

You can opt to have smart plugs turned on/off from within your Routine, handy for things like lamps (without smart bulbs), games consoles, kettles and more.

Speakers/music

As part of a recent update, you can now add music, podcasts and radio into a Routine. That's a big part of making improved wake up and bed time recipes.

Delaying steps with the 'Wait' option

You can also add in a 'wait option', which lets you add a block of time between steps - so you could have the alarm wake you up at 7am for example, with your favorite radio station, but then delay the lights coming on, and the kettle firing up, until 7.15am

Other types of Alexa action

News – You can have Alexa read you your flash briefing, which is made up of news skills. It's like getting a personalized news bullet-in to your tastes.

Weather – Get Alexa to read you the weather, probably best as part of a wake-up Routine. Remember, these can be timed to go off with your alarm, and if you get your coffee machine hooked up to a smart plug, you're onto a winner.

Calendar - Alexa will go over your calendar, whether it's today or tomorrow. You can also set it up to tell you the next event on your docket.

Messaging - No, Alexa isn't going to text for you. Instead, you can get Alexa to send you a notification via the Alexa app or send an announcement via Echo devices.

Traffic – Get a traffic report for your commute in. Again, best as part of a morning Routine.

Music - Alexa will play a song of your choice, which is great for when you need a certain song to get you in the mood for something. For instance, you could say "Alexa, pump me up" and have that link to Eye of the Tiger. You'll be able to choose the playing song from a number of music services, like Pandora, TuneIn, iHeartRadio and Amazon Music.

Alexa says – This is slightly weird, but you can get Alexa to say a phrase as part of a Routine. Choices include saying 'goodnight' or 'good morning', eight different happy birthday messages and a bunch of compliments, that are frankly bizarre.

How to Connect an Amazon Echo to a Harmony Remote

The Logitech Harmony Elite universal remote control, as well as other Harmony remotes, can control a range of smart home devices. For instance, you can connect your TV to your Apple TV and your stereo for the ultimate home theater. You can also link the commands and activities you create for the remote to your Amazon Echo.

Bear in mind that the only things you'll be able to control using Alexa are activities you've already created on the Harmony remote, so make sure you've completed that step before connecting it to the Amazon Echo.

1. Open the Alexa app, and select Skills & Games from the Home menu (press the three horizontal buttons on the top left).

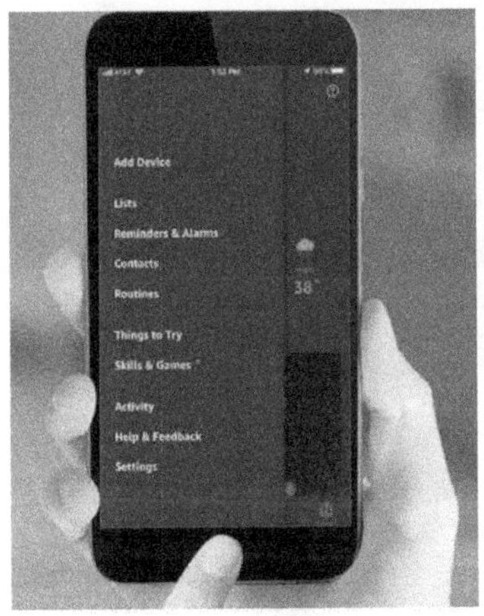

2. Search for "Harmony" and select the result with the blue Harmony logo.

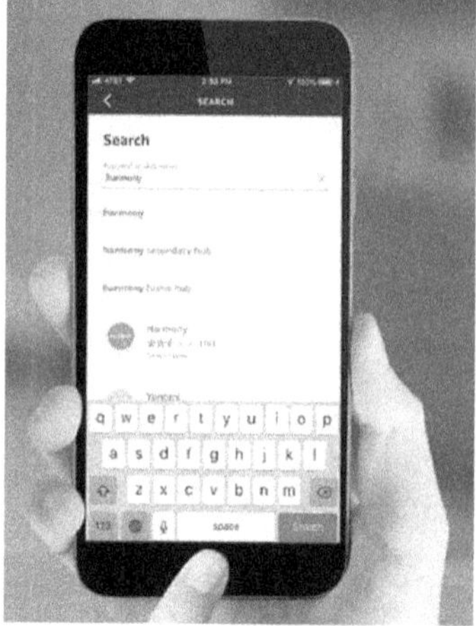

3. Enable the Harmony skill.

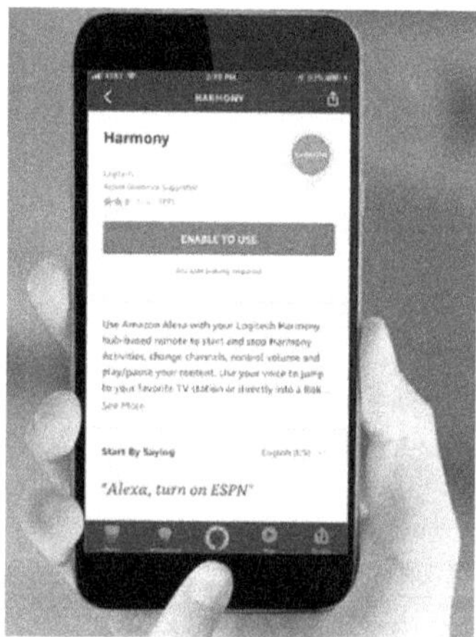

4. Login to your Logitech Harmony account.

5. Select the activities you wish to control using Alexa. You can also choose the wording to activate a particular activity.

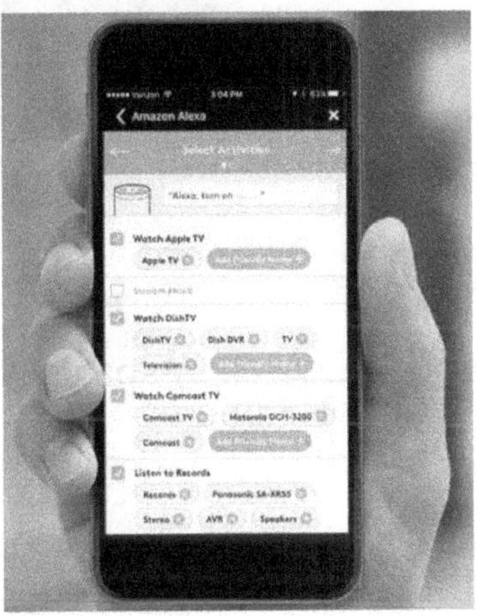

7. Select the TV stations you wish to control using Alexa. This way, you can simply say "Alexa, turn on

ESPN," and it will automatically change the channel for you.

8. Press Link Account to finish connecting Alexa to your Harmony remote.

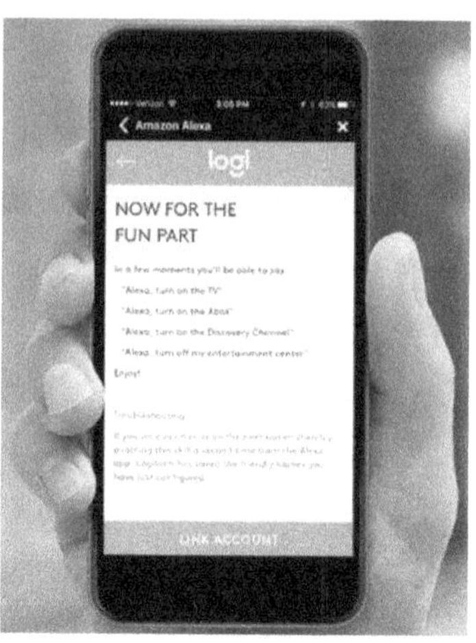

How to create an Amazon Echo stereo pair

Stereo pairing is a trick used by many manufacturers, letting you use two wireless speakers, one for the left channel and one for the right channel. With the Google Home Max, Apple HomePod and a range of Sonos speakers, such as the Sonos One, supporting stereo pairing, it was only a matter of time before Amazon got in on the act. Here's how to create an Amazon Echo stereo pair.

Before you start, it's essential that you have two of the same type of speaker. You can't mix and match your models or generations of speakers. For the latest generation that's two Echo Dot (3rd Gen), two Echo or two Echo Plus (2nd Gen) speakers that you'll need. The original Echo Plus is supported, but older products aren't. Once you've got two connected to your account, here's what you need to do.

1. Start the stereo pairing mode

Open the Amazon Alexa app and tap the control icon at the bottom right of the screen, then select one of the Amazon Echo speakers that you want to control. In the Connected Devices section you'll see Stereo Pair / Subwoofer, so select this option. Read the next page of advice and, when ready, tap Next to continue.

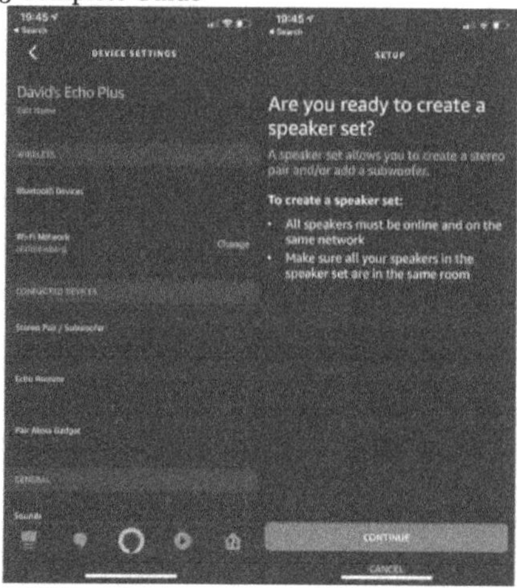

2. Choose your speakers

Next, select two speakers of the same type from the list of your Amazon Echo devices. Once you choose the first one, the only choices not greyed out will be the speakers that you can choose. Tap the next button.

You'll see the name of one of the speakers at the top of the app, and a choice 'Left' or 'Right'. Annoyingly, Amazon can't play a sound out of the selected speaker to help you identify it, so you may have to guess (don't worry you can flip the choice later).

Once you've chosen, tap Next and the Amazon Alexa app will assign the channel you didn't choose to the other Echo speaker.

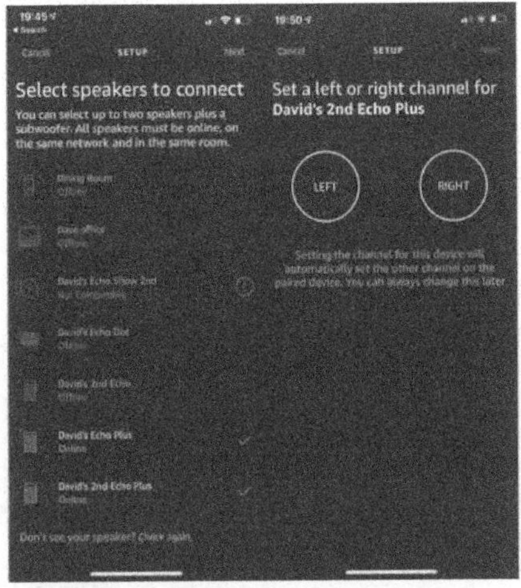

3. Finish the job

You'll see a progress bar as Alexa connects your two speakers. When done you'll get a new Stereo Pair listed, with the names of the two speakers that you used. Tap either speaker and you can choose which channel it is: left or right.

To get back to this screen, tap the Control icon in the Alexa app and you'll see your Stereo Pair listed under Speaker Groups. You can use the Delete Speaker Set option to split your two Echo devices apart.

When in a stereo pair, music will come out of both speakers, only one will act as the left channel and one the right channel. Volume control applies to both speakers. If you ask Alexa a question, just the speaker closest to you in the stereo pair will reply.

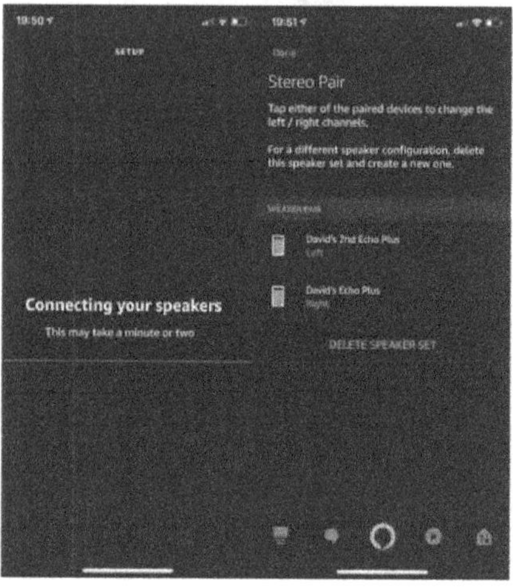

How to add an Amazon Echo Sub and configure Alexa EQ settings

The Amazon Echo Sub is a standalone product that adds extra bass to an existing Echo speaker. In this guide, we'll show you how to add an Amazon Echo Sub and configure Alexa EQ settings, so you can get the most out of the bass speaker.

You add an Echo Sub in the same way as any speaker. When you first add the speaker, Alexa will take you through the pairing process with another Echo Speaker (or two for a stereo pair). If you've already created a stereo pair, you first have to delete that pair. We'll show you how to add the Sub manually.

Finally, you need a supported Echo device. The current list of supported devices includes the Amazon Echo (1st Gen), Amazon Echo (2nd Gen), Echo Dot (3rd Gen), Echo Plus (1st Gen), Echo Plus (2nd Gen), Echo Show (1st Gen) and Echo Show (2nd Gen). Only the Echo (2nd Gen), Echo Dot (3rd Gen) and either generation Echo Plus can be used as a stereo pair with the Sub.

Step 1 – Create a speaker group with the sub

Open the Alexa app and tap the control icon at the bottom right of the screen. Tap the Plus icon and, from the menu that appears, pick the Add Stereo Pair / Subwoofer option. Read the instructions to make sure your speakers are in the right state for pairing and then tap Continue.

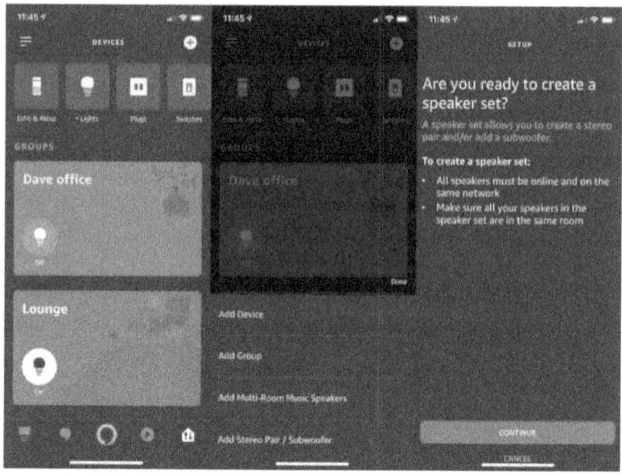

Step 2 – Select the speakers to use

From the list of your Echo speakers, tap the Echo Sub first. This will change the list above, so that you can only select the speakers that are compatible with the Sub. You can select one or two speakers from the list. The latter creates a stereo pair and only works if you select two speakers of the same type from this list. When done tap Next and the speaker group will be created.

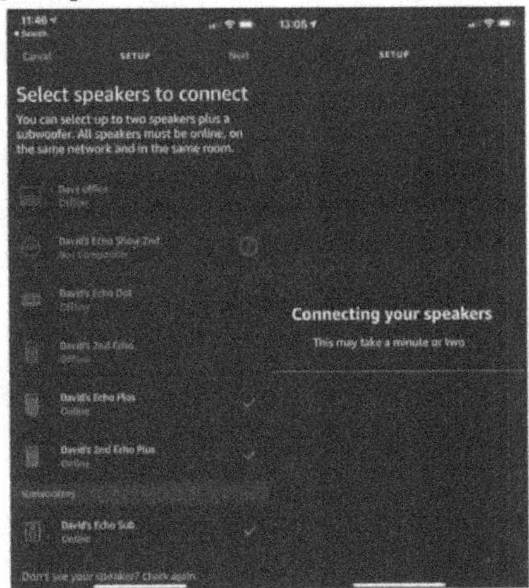

Step 3 – Manage Alexa EQ settings

You can adjust the sound of your speakers using the EQ settings. Go to the Alexa app and tap the control icon (bottom right). Then tap Echo & Alexa and select one of the Echo speakers that's in a speaker group with the Sub; note you can't get to the EQ if you pick the Sub.

Tap Sound under General and then select Equalizer under Media. You can use the sliders to increase or decrease the Bass, Midrange or Treble. Tap the back arrow when you're done. Note that EQ changes apply to all speakers in a group.

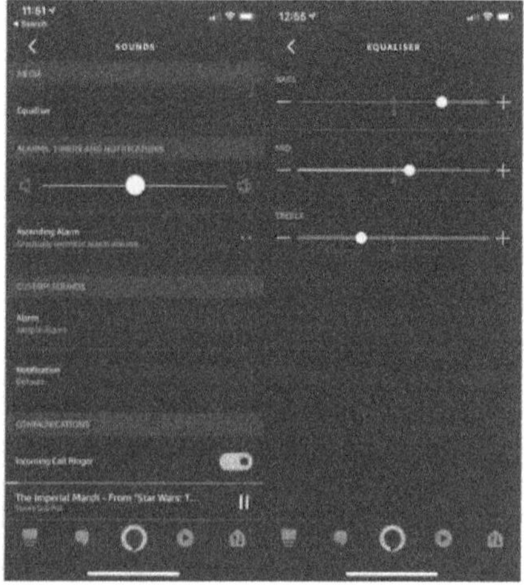

Step 4 – Delete the Sub pairing

If you want to attach the Echo Sub to a different product, you have to delete the pairing first. Go to the Alexa app and tap the control icon (bottom right) and select your speaker group from the bottom of the page. Tap Delete Speaker Set and you're done.

Creating an Amazon Household

The Amazon Echo Show is a fantastic tool for using your voice to manage everything from a shopping list to music playlist and to videos, but what if there are other people in your household? For people with multi-person households, especially where members of that household all have purchased various content on Amazon like music and audiobooks, then it makes a lot of sense to enabled shared profiles so that you can listen to each other's music. In addition to sharing music, you can also share shopping lists, to-dos, calendar entries, and other features available on the Echo/Alexa system. Let's us look at how you can add a profile to your Amazon Echo Show. All these actions can be performed by visiting echo.amazon.com, or through the Alexa App on your smart device. To add someone using the App, go to the menu sidebar and select **Settings**, under Settings select **Accounts** and choose **Household profiles,** you will then need to follow the on-screen instructions. Also, know that the person you desire to add may needs to be present to input their credentials.

Another method is to go to amazon.com and select **Accounts & Lists** near the top of the page, then select "Your Account." Go to the bottom right and select **shopping programs and rentals**, then select **Amazon Households.** Then select your desired option, **add adult**, **add** a **teen** and **add a child,** to follow the instructions.

Alexa App Home Page

You can view the App layout at alexa.amazon .com. Basically, the menu of app pages is on the left and the current page will be on the right. Also, you can see this display in large mobile devices, but the three horizontal lines which is depicted as the Menu, and the current page is what is normally displayed on most phones and tablets. At the top of the Home page, it will display **things to try, your cards** and the recent **music player**.

Things to try: this feature appears at the top of the Alexa App Home page. It rotates through some suggestions about 7-9 seconds of things you can say to Alexa, and these suggestions are mostly the trending or current issues. Below the suggestions there are shaded buttons, I normally tap through them to see the suggestions since I don't have the patience to wait for them rotate. There are few times I find things of interest at the suggestion, but when I don't see any, I focus on more important things than wasting time.

Player: When you load your media either playing or paused, you will see a player at the bottom of the app Home page. This allows you to control it, and you will see in the bar an icon of the current song in the queue. What I love about the player feature is that any page you are on, it will always display at the bottom of the App.

Cards: you create a card base on the frequent verbal interaction with Alexa. The primarily purpose of the card is to preserves the request and response from Alexa such as music station, videos, or forecast requested, and some items you added to your shopping list. All these things mentioned and other most verbal interactions form your card and the card forms your Alexa Dialog History. You scroll down to access the card or go through **settings** and select **history.**

Card options: you will see the top card in your history with several options:

- **Remove card:** This option is used to delete the card

- **Give voice feedback:** This feature is use to access the questions or commands you gave to Alexa and the feedback received. You will be able to know if Alexa is giving you the right answer or not, and you can give your feedback with "Yes" or "No." However, if you are unsatisfied with Alexa response, kindly answer "No" and an option to send more detailed feedback to Amazon will be given to you. If Alexa is not carrying out your instruction, you can can do a voice training by going to **Settings>Accounts> Voice Training**

- **Learn More:** The learn more option will take you to Alexa, and Alexa Device FAQs, which serves as another crucial part of the Help & Feedback section Menu. I will advice you check them out when you are less busy.

Note: you can only delete your entire history by deregistering your device. I sometimes use this feature when I want to give away my device as a gift or sell it out. However, you can choose to deregister and reregister your device. Check the settings section to see more explanation.

- **Wikipedia & Bing Search:** one or both of these search engine options might appear on a card. There are times the Card displayed a short answer and the link to the subject on Wikipedia, but this depends on the topic you asked Alexa about. Also, Alexa might be unclear about what you asked and it will give you the option to search Bing for that person, place, thing or whatever your query was about. The only search engine option on the app is Bing.

How to set up and use Alexa Drop In and Calling

Alexa is a brilliant communicator, and is loaded with features for talking to your friends and family. Drop In and Alexa Announcements make a great home intercom system, and you can use Alexa Calling to make phone calls, too.

Amazon's Alexa enables you to speak to anyone in the home – to see what time dinner's ready, whether the kids are in from school, or even to demand the delivery of a cup of tea upstairs. You can Drop In from work or the pub using your smartphone or through rooms via Amazon Echo devices and even Fire tablets in Show mode.

And what's more – it's not even confined to your own home. You can Drop In on friends and relatives with Alexa, or if they're not ready to have you appear in their living rooms unchecked, use Alexa Calling instead.

Alexa Announcements, meanwhile, is a feature that lets you broadcast messages to your Echo speakers without the right to reply - so, let's explore how to set it all up.

What is Alexa Drop In and how do you enable it?

Drop In enables you call up one of the Alexa devices from within your household. It can be used to check in with home, rather than calling specific people, or as an intercom between Alexa devices in other rooms, which can be handy, especially in larger homes. If your contact has an Echo Show or Echo Spot, you can drop in via video as well.

While Drop In has become somewhat of a catch-all term when it comes to calling Alexa devices, it generally only really applies to your Echo speakers registered to your Alexa app. However, friends and family can allow you to Drop In on them, too. That means you will connect to their device to chat via two-way audio/video at will, without them answering/accepting the call.

How do you sign up?

We're going to assume that you've got the Alexa app downloaded and got your Amazon Echo all hooked up. So the next thing to do is sign up for Alexa Calling and Messaging, which you do in the Alexa app. At the bottom, tap the Conversations tab, denoted by that little speech bubble, and sign up.

How to start a Drop In from your Alexa device

You don't have to do all this from a smartphone, and, naturally, you can ask Alexa to Drop In on a device. To do this just say, "Alexa, Drop In on [insert the name of your speaker]," to start a call. This only works for devices   within   your   home   -   to   Drop   In   on wider contacts, things are done slightly differently.

How to Drop In on friends and family

Providing your contacts have approved you for Drop In, you can say, "Alexa, Drop In on [contact name]". Just make sure you name them as they appear in your address book. If you're using a device with a screen, like Echo Show, the video is distorted for a few seconds then good to go - if you want to turn it off say, "Alexa, video off," or touch the screen and select it that way.

Also worth noting: if you don't want people Dropping In on you right now - secret business - then enable Do Not Disturb on your Echo - just saying, "Alexa, don't disturb me," will do the trick.

How to start a Drop In from the Alexa app

To Drop In to a contact from your smartphone, just head to the Alexa app and go to the Conversations tab. You'll see a big Drop In tab, which you tap to see a quick list of all Alexa devices you're cleared to access. If, for whatever reason, you can't see the one you're looking for, you can hit the contact icon at the top right, choose the person from your address book and Drop In from there.

How to view security camera footage

Did you know that you can watch a live feed of your smart security camera on your Amazon Echo Show, Echo Spot, or even your TV if you've got an Amazon Fire stick?

It's a simple thing to set up and it means that you can create a security monitor without ever firing up your smartphone or tablet. All you need is one of the three Amazon devices noted in the intro and a compatible smart security camera.

Obviously, with Google owning Nest, you can also Chromecast your Nest security camera footage too - but that's a different story.

Security cameras that work with Alexa

The Alexa compatible security cameras that will display their feeds on an Echo Show, Spot or Fire TV are from the following brands: Nest, Netgear Arlo, Ring, Logitech, TP-Link, Honeywell, Wyze, Ezviz, Amcrest and, of course, the Amazon Cloud Cam works too.

Beware of skills for other security camera brands you see listed in the Alexa app – unless they are from the ones we've listed above the voice controls will be limited to turning them on and off, checking the status and so on.

Connect your security in the Alexa app

- Go to the menu and tap Skills.

- Find the relevant skill (some cameras have specific apps for the cameras, outside of their main smart home apps).

- Enable the skill and link the account with Alexa.

- Add the camera as a device, using the 'Add Device' button in the smart home section or by asking, "Alexa, discover my devices."

Show your security camera using Alexa

- The command to see the stream is, "Alexa, show [camera name]". The camera name is the one you have listed in the Alexa app. By default it will use the name from the camera's parent app but you can change it. To view the name for your camera in the Alexa app, go to the menu and select Smart Home > Devices.

- If you have linked an Echo speaker to a Fire TV

device, you can say the command to that in order to see the feed on your TV (or speak through the remote control).

- To stop watching, simply say: "Alexa, hide [camera name],""Alexa, stop," "Alexa, go home," "Alexa, show the homescreen," or "Alexa, show the clock," (on a Show or Spot).

- You can also press the back button on a Fire TV remote or the Echo screen to exit.

- The feed stays on for a time determined by the camera maker – it's 30 minutes on Nest, for example. You have to ask Alexa to show it again once the time is up.

How to set up and use Alexa Drop In and Calling

Alexa is a brilliant communicator, and is loaded with features for talking to your friends and family. Drop In and Alexa Announcements make a great home intercom system, and you can use Alexa Calling to make phone calls, too.

Amazon's Alexa enables you to speak to anyone in the home – to see what time dinner's ready, whether the kids are in from school, or even to demand the delivery of a cup of tea upstairs. You can Drop In from work or the pub using your smartphone or through rooms via Amazon Echo devices and even Fire tablets in Show mode.

And what's more – it's not even confined to your own home. You can Drop In on friends and relatives with Alexa, or if they're not ready to have you appear in their living rooms unchecked, use Alexa Calling instead.

Alexa Announcements, meanwhile, is a feature that lets you broadcast messages to your Echo speakers without the right to reply - so, let's explore how to set it all up.

What is Alexa Drop In and how do you enable it?

Drop In enables you call up one of the Alexa devices from within your household. It can be used to check in with home, rather than calling specific people, or as an intercom between Alexa devices in other rooms, which can be handy, especially in larger homes. If your contact has an Echo Show or Echo Spot, you can drop in via video as well.

While Drop In has become somewhat of a catch-all term when it comes to calling Alexa devices, it generally only really applies to your Echo speakers registered to your Alexa app. However, friends and family can allow you to Drop In on them, too. That means you will connect to their device to chat via two-way audio/video at will, without them answering/accepting the call.

How do you sign up?

We're going to assume that you've got the Alexa app downloaded and got your Amazon Echo all hooked up. So the next thing to do is sign up for Alexa Calling and Messaging, which you do in the Alexa app. At the bottom, tap the Conversations tab, denoted by that little speech bubble, and sign up.

How to start a Drop In from your Alexa device

You don't have to do all this from a smartphone, and, naturally, you can ask Alexa to Drop In on a device. To do this just say, "Alexa, Drop In on [insert the name of your speaker]," to start a call. This only works for devices within your home - to Drop In on wider contacts, things are done slightly differently.

How to Drop In on friends and family

Providing your contacts have approved you for Drop In, you can say, "Alexa, Drop In on [contact name]". Just make sure you name them as they appear in your address book. If you're using a device with a screen, like Echo Show, the video is distorted for a few seconds then good to go - if you want to turn it off say, "Alexa, video off," or touch the screen and select it that way.

Also worth noting: if you don't want people Dropping In on you right now - secret business - then enable Do

Not Disturb on your Echo - just saying, "Alexa, don't disturb me," will do the trick.

How to start a Drop In from the Alexa app

To Drop In to a contact from your smartphone, just head to the Alexa app and go to the Conversations tab. You'll see a big Drop In tab, which you tap to see a quick list of all Alexa devices you're cleared to access. If, for whatever reason, you can't see the one you're looking for, you can hit the contact icon at the top right, choose the person from your address book and Drop In from there.

How to view security camera footage

Did you know that you can watch a live feed of your smart security camera on your Amazon Echo Show, Echo Spot, or even your TV if you've got an Amazon Fire stick?

It's a simple thing to set up and it means that you can create a security monitor without ever firing up your smartphone or tablet. All you need is one of the three

Amazon devices noted in the intro and a compatible smart security camera.

Obviously, with Google owning Nest, you can also Chromecast your Nest security camera footage too - but that's a different story.

Security cameras that work with Alexa

The Alexa compatible security cameras that will display their feeds on an Echo Show, Spot or Fire TV are from the following brands: Nest, Netgear Arlo, Ring, Logitech, TP-Link, Honeywell, Wyze, Ezviz, Amcrest and, of course, the Amazon Cloud Cam works too.

Beware of skills for other security camera brands you see listed in the Alexa app – unless they are from the ones we've listed above the voice controls will be limited to turning them on and off, checking the status and so on.

Connect your security in the Alexa app

- Go to the menu and tap Skills.

- Find the relevant skill (some cameras have specific apps for the cameras, outside of their main smart home apps).

- Enable the skill and link the account with Alexa.

- Add the camera as a device, using the 'Add Device' button in the smart home section or by asking, "Alexa, discover my devices."

Show your security camera using Alexa

- The command to see the stream is, "Alexa, show [camera name]". The camera name is the one you have listed in the Alexa app. By default it will use the name from the camera's parent app but you can change it. To view the name for your camera in the Alexa app, go to the menu and select Smart Home > Devices.

- If you have linked an Echo speaker to a Fire TV device, you can say the command to that in order to see the feed on your TV (or speak through the remote control).

- To stop watching, simply say: "Alexa, hide [camera name],""Alexa, stop," "Alexa, go home," "Alexa, show the homescreen," or "Alexa, show the clock," (on a Show or Spot).

- You can also press the back button on a Fire TV remote or the Echo screen to exit.

- The feed stays on for a time determined by the camera maker – it's 30 minutes on Nest, for example. You have to ask Alexa to show it again once the time is up.

Watching Videos with the Echo Show

With the introduction of the Echo Show, you can now watch your favorite videos. However, the Echo Show is not like your TV in the sitting room, so don't expect a high resolution for movies or music videos, but it is pretty good. This 7-inch screen can be use to watch videos from Amazon and YouTube. If you have an Amazon Video account- also an account with all of Amazon streaming channels such as Showtime, Starz,

Cinemax, HBO and host of others- you can command the device (Alexa) to display the videos on your video library or play a video from a specific watch list. Alexa Video also supports Fire TV and Dish TV, and all these will be explain below.

How to Watch Amazon Video on Echo Show

You can use the Echo Show device to watch huge offering of digital movies and TV shows from Amazon Video by issuing your command word, "Alexa, show me funny cat videos. You can obtain video from three sources:

- **Amazon prime membership and prime for students:** This is an amazing offer that I love so much. Being a member, you can gain access to thousands of video titles for movies; TV shows, and Amazon original content are available at no extra cost with a prime trial or membership. For more details and the offer, kindly go to amazon.com and select Amazon video department, then go to the tab that says

included with prime and all the details will be there for you to follow.

- **Amazon video:** This feature allows you to see the digital version of movies, TV shows and series and any other video content that you personally download from Amazon to form your Video Library.

- **Video subscriptions:** As mentioned previously, Amazon streaming channels like Showtime, HBO, Starz and other free niche genres are not free. You need to subscribe for these third-party channels before you can have access to their services. To view these third-party services, kindly click the **channels** tab on the Amazon video page.

Now that you have gotten what to watch on your Echo Show device, let us look at various ways you can gain access.

- **Search your library**: You can ask Alexa, "Show me my watchlist or my video library" and you will see it display on the screen. You can then swipe through the screen to make a selection.

- **Show by actor genre**: This is another way you can access what you want to watch by mentioning the name of the author or the genre. For example, you can tell Alexa, "Show me Kenneth Dick movies," or "Show me animated movies," and Alexa will tell you, "Here is what I found." The search result will display on the screen, you can then scroll through to make your selection.

- **Search by title:** you can also search by title by giving a command of the movie title to Alexa and it will show on the screen. Once any of your desired content is being shown on the device, there are two ways you can control it:

1. **Use voice to issue common commands:** The primarily way to use the Echo Show is to issue command via speech. In as much as the device has a touchscreen where you can navigate to different sections, you are meant to issue

command and not get acquainted with the touch screen. Issue these common commands once the video is playing:

- Play/pause/resume

- Rewind/fast forward

- Go back/skip ahead and number of seconds, minutes or hours

- Next video/next episode

When you give Alexa these commands it will do as you have spoken.

2. **Tap the Echo Show screen:** This is the common method that we are use to over the years. I sometimes use the touchscreen of my Alexa because I am now used to touchscreen devices like Kindle and Smartphone. Therefore, tap play/pause and other symbols on the screen.

Watch Movie Trailers on Echo Show

You can watch any movie trailer from IMDB on Echo Show by simply saying, "Show me the movie trailer for [movie title]."

There are two ways you can control the trailer playback:

- Tap the Echo Show screen to view and use the limited player that includes pause/play and symbols of going forward/back 10 seconds
- Use voice with common commands like:
  - Play/pause/resume
  - Rewind/fast forward
  - Go back/skip ahead and number of seconds

When it comes to watching movie trailers on Echo Show, it is what I am really delighted about. These kinds of short video content are super amazing on the small Echo Show screen. I prefer using my TV to watch TV series and Movies because of the larger screen.

However, using the Alexa to operate the Fire TV is also amazing.

Using Echo Show to Operate Fire TV

Yes, it is possible to control your Fire TV with Alexa. The Fire TV is a comprehensive media and personal assistant center that can be paired with and controlled by any Echo device. To be candid, you need to buy one of the Fire TV device options before you can use your Fire TV with the Echo Show device.

You can view most streaming and live TV series with Fire TV including HBO Now, NBA, Hulu, Netflix, Comedy Central, CNN, MLB.TV, Sling, DirectTV Now, and Amazon. All these and some others are things you can watch with Fire TV.

Some other things you can do with Fire TV and Alexa is to enjoy music services played via your equipment such as Amazon music, and iHeartRadio, play games, order an Uber or pizza and many other stuff. I will advise you search through Amazon to see what your Fire TV offers.

How to Connect Alexa and Fire TV

Let me give you a quick rundown on how this can easily be done. However, some instructions are provided by Amazon on how you can set up Fire TV equipment and how you can make the most of it. Follow these instructions on how you can control Fire TV with Alexa:

- In the Alexa App, go to **Music, Video & Books** and select **Fire TV**

- Select **Link Your Alexa Device** and choose the device you want to use

- You will see onscreen prompts; follow it to complete the process. Once you are through with the setup process, you can engage Alexa with the following request:
  - "Watch Law and Order"
  - "Show me Michael Dick movies"
  - "Next episode"

- o "Jump to 30 minutes"

- o "Rewind 5 minutes"

- o Order Domino's pizza"

- o Much, much, more!

In conclusion, when your Echo Show device is linked to your Fire TV, you are able to control the Fire TV options on your TV. However, you can't watch programs directly on your Echo Show screen.

Connecting Alexa to Dish TV

If you have a Dish TV, you can link it to Alexa. There is a cordial relationship between the two but the requirements are Dish TV Package, and DISH Hopper Smart DVR. The devices currently supported are Hopper with Sling, Hopper and Wally, and Hopper 3 and Newer.

The benefits of liking your Dish TV is that you can ask Alexa to play your recorded content, search for shows, movies or actors, change the channel (ex. "Go to channel 55"), pause, rewind, fast-forward, etc. it is really cool when you start using your voice to control these features.

How to setup Dish TV on Alexa

The process of doing this is not as complicated as many thought. The first thing you need to do is to go to **music, videos & books**, then select **Dish TV**, and enable the skill. Before you proceed, ensure your Amazon login credentials are with you because it might be needed during the setup process. After you have enabled the skill, onscreen directions will be displayed, kindly follow these directions or instructions to connect Alexa to Dish TV. Some of these instructions are, turning on your Hopper setup box and TV, then a code will be given on the TV screen, ensure you enter it into the Alexa App and select **finish setup** in the Alexa App.

Note: the Hopper's software might need to be updated to the latest version before the Dish TV can be used with Alexa. You can do this update by going to your Dish set-top box, navigate to channel 9607 and select

software update so that your receiver can be updated to the latest software. Make sure you allow the updating process to complete and the Hopper box to restart before continuing the linking process on the Alexa App.

Playing Music Unlimited With The Echo Show

The echo Show is awesome when it comes to playing music. What I love about this device is the ability to play from a diverse range of sources such as: my music library, Amazon music, Spotify, Pandora, iHeartRadio, Tunein, SiriusXm and listen to audiobooks. Do you see why I said this device is awesome! We will look at how you can play music from these various sources.

My Music Library

In this section of the App, you are able to access your personal music collections. But the **Amazon music** section is where you can access all the available music in Amazon. Wow! Personally, I always use my music Library because I got a lot of cool stuff there, and it is a large Library of music. Your Music Library is made up of:

- Music purchased from Amazon

- Selections from Amazon Prime and Amazon Music Unlimited subscription

- Imported: Uploaded playlist from different sources such as Google play, iTunes, etc. to your My Music account on Amazon.

You can upload music to your library either from your PC or MAC, go to music.amazon.com/home and select **imported** from My Music, then choose **upload your music** box. You can upload or import up to 250 songs to Amazon cloud for free. **Note**: You might be asked to install the Amazon Music for PC/MAC during the process, kindly does that. If the Amazon free cloud storage is too small for your music storage, you can subscribe for Amazon Music storage at the rate of $24.99 yearly, then you can import up to 250, 000 songs. You can check details by going to your Amazon account and selecting **Amazon Music Settings>Music Storage.**

Amazon Prime/Amazon Music Unlimited

Since we are still in the discussion of music, I will like to clarify the difference between the Amazon Prime/Amazon Music Unlimited. Personally, I love the prime membership a lot because it offers a lot of benefits such as:

- 2 million+ songs in prime music with so many shipping, shopping benefits on Amazon
- Student Annual fee-$49 after a 6-month free trial
- Standard monthly fee-$10.99
- Standard annual fee-$99 after a 30-day free trial

The Amazon Music Unlimited offers you the benefits of "Tens of millions of songs," that is what Amazon said. But have you ever sit down to ask yourself how long it will take you to play thirty thousand songs, let alone millions of songs. Well, if you love music so much, you can consider the Amazon Music Unlimited with a monthly fee of $3.99 after 30-day free trial; this package is for Echo devices.

PANDORA

If you have a free Pandora account, you can use the Alexa Echo Show. However, Pandora has three membership levels:

- Pandora free: you will get free Ad-supported radio, and personalized stations

- Pandora plus: this comes with a fee of $4.99 monthly, 30-day free trial, Ad-free Personalized stations, Offline radio, and Better audio.

- Pandora premium: in this plan, you must pay a monthly fee of $9.99, including 60-day free trial, Ad-free, you don't need to personalize existing stations but creating new stations and playlist, Better audio, you can download music to other devices, and there is no limit on skips and replays. You can get more information about their membership packages at Pandora.com.

Spotify

This is one of the largest music streaming platforms with a total of about 140 million users and 50 million subscribers. Spotify has a free subscription, but you need a premium account which is approximately ten dollars monthly to use it with the Echo Show. There are other benefits that go with the premium account which include the ability to download music to your device to listen offline, play any song and listen without ads, and you can skip songs that you don't like. If you wish to create an account with them, have an email address, password, username, and a payment method (PayPal or credit card). You can get more details about this by visiting spotify.com

How to link Alexa to Spotify

After you have subscribed for the premium account, go to **music, video & books**, select **spotify>link your account> authorize the account** (If Requested). Once this process is done, you will see a new window pop up where you are asked to authorize the connection of Alexa to your Spotify account. After the authorization, go to the Alexa app and you will be asked if you want to make Spotify your default music service. You can choose to say "Yes" or "No." the advantage of making Spotify as your default music service is that you can easily request music from your favorite artist and Alexa will play it instantly. For instance, you can tell Alexa, "Play Jay Z" and it will play it instantly but if Spotify is not your default settings, you need to be specific. For example, "Play Jay Z on Spotify."

However, you can always change your music default service anytime. Kindly go to **settings>music & media> choose default music services.** Now that you have successfully link Alexa to Spotify, always issue a command to Alexa so that you can enjoy the music on this platform.

iHeartRadio

This radio platform has a large amount of music and podcasts which is provided by 800 iHeartRadio partner stations in the US, and a range of other media. It also has over a thousand artist stations. This platform offers three level of membership:

- **iHeartRadio**: this level of membership has zero cost, but it has a limitation of choosing a local radio station or selected stations built around well-known artists.

- **iHeartRadio Plus**: To be a member of this package, you are required to pay approximately five dollars monthly and you will have some interesting features such as replaying the last three songs you listened to on a live radio station, you have the ability to save a song to your favorite to play it again later. You also have the option of searching for a particular artist and immediately play those tracks, finally, you can skip songs an unlimited number of times but it only works when you are listening to a custom radio station.

- **iHeartRadio All Access**: you pay approximately ten dollars monthly for membership and you will have everything offered in plus including unlimited access to millions, build playlists, and most importantly, listen offline. You can try anyone of this paid plan and enjoyed your Alexa with it.

How to Link Alexa to iHeartRadio

There is nothing complicated about this, it is the same process mentioned previously with Spotify. Just go to your Music, Video & Books page and select iHeartRadio, then link your account. You can authorize the link to an existing account or create a free or upgraded account.

How to use iHeartRadio on Echo Show

There is a search box on the home page where you can type in artist name or keywords. Searches return results related to your keyword, and they are divided into four categories: the **stations**, **songs**, **artists**, and **talkshows**. All these options can be used to locate your desired. You can also try the second option by browsing through the section where you have three categories. The first category is the **live radio**- you can access over 800 radio sections from all over the country. You have the **shows** sections where you can have access to podcast including business & finance, entertainment, crime, politics, spirituality, sports etc. The last category is the **favorites**. You can choose any show or station as your favorite and it will be saved there for easy access later.

You can manually choose any station and it will start playing or you can use your voice to command Alexa of what you want but you must be specific.

SiriusXM

Linking your Alexa to SiriusXm is another unique way you can enjoy your device. This platform has an online radio with over 70 music channels, over 20 talk and entertainment channels, 15+ news and issues channels, 10+ channels, you have traffic and weather and a lot more. However, with all these benefits, Alexa & SiriusXM connection is problematic and complicated.

There are a lot of complaints from users about accessing SirusXM, that Alexa can't recognize login information and so many other things. You can find out more details on the SiriusXm page and you will also see the rating.

Personally, I didn't link My Alexa to SiriusXm due to the fact that I can't search or browse from the Alexa App. The only option available when I tried it last is to use your voice, and that means you must know the name of what you want to hear.

Tunein

Tunein was founded in 2002 and it has been one of the oldest streaming services with areas of specialties such as sports, music, news and talk. It has the free and premium accounts. With the free account, you can stream over 600 radio stations. If you want the premium account, a monthly fee of approximately ten dollars is requested and you will have access to over 600 radio stations and 40,000 audio books.

How to link Alexa to Tunein

The process remains the same as the previous ones. Go to **Music**, **Video & Books** page and select **Tunein > Link your account > Authorized the link.** You can set up an account there and select the level of membership you want by providing your standard and payment information.

How to Use Tunein on Echo Show?

The Tunein homepage has a **search box** just like the iHeartRadio page. If you want to use the search box, you need to be more specific by typing in the exact name of the show or your desired station, otherwise the search box returns uncategorized results, and it is always a headache for me going through a very long list of results. Therefore, you got to be specific to get a better search result.

Another method is to use the **browse** function which I prefer to the former. You can select:

- o Sports with over 20 subcategories.

- o By language with over 90 languages

- o Podcasts- which is divided into talk, sports and music categories and various subcategories

- o Location- you are able to find news from continents and regions.

- o News that are trending from popular sources like CNN, BCC and host of others

- o Talk- over 30 genre subcategories that you can browse through.

- o Music- this contains over 40 subcategories

- o Local Radio- this is base on your location during Echo Show setup.

- o Favorites-this contains the content you like.

You can go through all these categories or subcategories from search or by browsing through them. Sometimes, browsing through the App seems best for me because if I use voice command, Alexa sometimes finds it a bit difficult to bring out my request. We are through with this part. Don't forget that on the **music & books page** of the App, you have audible and kindle. That is the next thing we will look at.

How Alexa Brief Mode Works

As most Alexa users will attest, it can be a little grating how verbose Amazon's voice assistant can be – so enter Brief Mode, which cuts down on Alexa's little chats.

When you're an experienced user, you don't require the level of confirmation feedback that Alexa tends to offer. But there's a solution on the way - Amazon is currently rolling out Brief Mode, its latest feature that aims to make Alexa even easier to live with.

Once enabled, this reduces the verbal feedback from Alexa, and in many instances, replaces it altogether with a beep. That should be enough to confirm that Alexa has heard and understood your request, without the verbal bombardment.

Alexa Brief Mode: UK, Germany and France

Brief Mode started rolling out to devices back in April, but was limited to the US. We can now confirm that Brief Mode is landing in the UK, Germany and France. It's landing slower than previous Alexa features. So don't worry if you don't see it in your Alexa settings menu – it is coming, just in its own sweet time.

However, it seems to be working differently in the new territories (for now). Alexa will tell you that Brief Mode is available, and ask you whether you want to enable it. You can say yes or no at this stage. However, the below steps don't yet apply. We're guessing that Amazon is waiting for the rollout to be completed before changing the app to reflect the feature.

How to turn on Brief Mode (US)

1. Open the Alexa app

2. Head to the Settings Menu

3. Scroll down to General

4. Look for Alexa Voice Responses

5. Turn on Brief Mode

Once enabled, Alexa should respond a little differently to your requests.

Those who use Alexa-compatible smart home devices will notice the most, as Brief Mode snuffs out those annoying "OK" responses every time you adjust the brightness of your living room lights. This will also extend to things like asking for music, where you don't have to get the full artist name, song, album and year of release repeated back to you with every request.

It should be pretty subtle, mind. You won't get a series of bleeps when you ask for a weather report, like a meteorological R2-D2 – but hopefully you should find Alexa more natural to live with.

How to play podcasts with Alexa on your Amazon Echo

If you're a fan of the latest and greatest podcasts, Alexa can be a great way to keep up with your favourite series. Alexa has the capability to play podcasts natively via TuneIn, but there's also a better way.

Play Alexa podcasts via TuneIn

Alexa defaults to the TuneIn skill for listening to podcasts, which has a decent selection of titles for you to subscribe and listen to.

Just head into the Amazon Alexa smartphone app and dive into the Music and Books section of the menu.

TuneIn is primarily a radio app, so you'll need to scroll all the way to the bottom to find the options for podcasting. Get the feeling that it's a bit of a forgotten feature? You might be right.

Once in the podcast section, you can search for what you want to subscribe to. Some ideas are provided for you, although these are hardly a cutting edge curation of the latest and greatest podcasts. In fact, the list is full of generic genres that just screams low quality.

But the selection is pretty good. Search for S-Town, Serial, The Butterfly Effect. When you find one you want, tap it to play on one of your Alexa devices.

Normally, at this stage, we'd recommend some Alexa commands for you to try – but sadly we found the entire process brutally awful to use, so we're not going to recommend any. You can't even subscribe to podcasts and Alexa is pretty rubbish at playing the correct episodes of serialized titles. But there is a better way...

Use AnyPod to play Podcasts with Alexa

The AnyPod skill is a much beefier podcast choice for Alexa that offers more options than the standard. To enable it, just say "Alexa, enable AnyPod skill."

The voice search works much better than via TuneIn, which really isn't set up for podcasts, and the whole process is easier and neater.

What's more, you can subscribe to a podcast, listen to your subscriptions, and AnyPod will work out the right episode for you to listen to. Listening to The Butterfly Effect took us to the first episode in the series, while a request for The Totally Football Show took us to the latest one. That's the kind of experience you need when controlling a service with your voice. We know you can't wait to get going, so here are the essential commands to get you started with AnyPod.

Play a podcast

"Alexa, ask AnyPod to play [name of podcast]."

Subscribe to a podcast

"Alexa, ask AnyPod to subscribe to [insert name of podcast]."

Play a specific episode:

"Alexa, ask AnyPod to play episode XX of [podcast name]."

Jump to the first or last episode

"Alexa, ask AnyPod for the [newest/oldest] episode."

List your podcast subscriptions:

"Alexa, ask AnyPod, 'What are my subscriptions?'"

Skip forward or back an episode

"Alexa, play the [next/previous] episode."

Add podcasts to Routines

Thanks to a recent update, you can now add Podcasts to your Alexa Routines – this means that with one single command you can control pretty much every aspect of your smart home, and play a podcast automatically.

To add a podcast to a Routine you must use the TuneIn skill – for now at least. That's slightly annoying, but until Amazon opens Routines up further, that's the way it is. Go to the app and choose Routines. Start a new Routine and choose the command you'll give Alexa – then go to Music, and choose TuneIn as the source.

Now it gets weird – you have to type in the name of the podcast you want to play manually. Once that's done, save the Routine and, of course, add any other smart home settings you want to run simultaneously – maybe you like to listen to your podcast in the warmth of a low, blueish hue. If you do, set this here. When you say the command, your podcast will play.

How to control your TV with Alexa

Yes, it's possible to control your TV with Alexa; Amazon Fire TV owners can control their streaming sticks using their Echo speakers.

If you've got an Echo Dot, Echo Show, Echo Spot or any other Echo speaker in the same room as the television you've got your Fire TV plugged into, you've got the option to control your viewing - or access your security camera feeds - using just your voice; there's no need to pick up that remote control.

Plus, if your TV supports HDMI-CEC, you'll also be able to power it on from standby simply by saying a Fire TV command such as, "Alexa, open Netflix".

It's super simple to get started. In fact, if you've only got one Fire TV device then by simply using a compatible command, you'll automatically pair an Echo device to it.

For example, if you've got an Echo Dot in your living room and you say, "Alexa, watch Midsomer Murders," then your Dot instantly pair up with the only Fire TV it can find in your Alexa account. You can only have one Fire TV paired to each Echo speaker - but you can have multiple Echos synced up with one Fire TV; handy if you've got a pair of Echo speakers either side of your couch, for example.

If you do have more than one Fire TV then you'll need to jump into the Alexa app to pair your devices:

- Select 'Music, Video, & Books'

- Choose your Fire TV

- Check the boxes of the Echo(s) that you want to control it

One interesting note is, while you can fire up a smart home security camera feed (from a Nest Cam, for example) by saying, "Alexa, show me the [room name]", if your paired Echo device has a screen - i.e. is a Show or Spot - that device will default as the playback device for that command.

Far-field control of Fire TV works on all generations of Fire TV and Fire TV Stick and all models of Echo speaker can be paired up.

Alexa Fire TV commands

Once synced up you'll have access to an absolute wealth of new Alexa commands, mostly focused on streaming TV, obviously - but there's also the security camera access we've already mentioned.

Here's some top Fire TV Alexa commands to try out. The results you will get on screen will depend what streaming apps you've installed on your Fire TV.

- "Alexa, watch [movie title]"

- "Alexa, pause"

- "Alexa, fast forward [x] minutes"

- "Alexa, rewind [x] seconds."

- "Alexa, next / next Episode."

- "Alexa, turn it down on Fire TV."

- "Alexa, show me movies with [actor's name]"

- "Alexa, open Netflix"

- "Alexa, show me popular show on [app]"

- "Alexa, go to [channel / network] on [app]."

How to add and control your lights and devices

Smart speakers are gateway devices, and are the key that unlocks easy control of the smart home. Research has shown that the preferred device of Amazon Alexa users is smart bulbs, followed by smart home hubs, thermostats and cameras. In this guide we look at how to connect your devices up with Alexa and how to control them.

Why connect your home with Alexa?

So first of all, why bother to go to the effort of buying Alexa compatible devices? Well, to put it succinctly, Alexa really starts to make sense in your home when controlling smart devices.

Alexa is extremely adept at making smart home tech work together. It's easy to set up single command groups that can control multiple lights, plugs and other devices together, which means a single command can set the mood in your entire house, be it walking in the door, getting ready for some TV time, or just switching everything off for bed time.

How to set up smart home devices in Alexa

The first bit comes down to following the instructions of the specific device. We'll take Philips Hue lights as an example. Before you get started you'll make sure the Philips Bridge is installed, that your lights are plugged into fittings and they're working properly within the Hue app.

That goes for any device – you'll need to install it properly first within its own app and ecosystem before you get going with Alexa.

The exception to this rule is if you're using the Amazon Echo Plus, which has the power to discover some smart home devices, if they use the Zigbee protocol. While this will need a little investigation on your part, Belkin WeMo, Honeywell thermostats, Ikea Tradfli, Philips Hue and Yale locks are all Zigbee.

How to add devices to Alexa

Unless you're using the Amazon Echo Plus, you're going to need to install Alexa skills for the devices you want Alexa to discover. This isn't a complicated process, but you will need the login info for each of the smart device ecosystems you're going to add.

That's because an Alexa skill effectively links your Amazon account to that of Lifx, Philips Hue, Hive,

Nest or whatever service you're using. The easiest way to install the Alexa skill is to go to the app, choose Skills from the list, and search for the brand. The app will take you through the process of adding your login details.

Once you've set your devices up in their own ecosystems, it's time to hook them up with Alexa. You can do this two ways: first you can just ask "Alexa discover my devices" or you can head to the Amazon Alexa app > Smart Home and press the + button in the top right (see above).

Alexa will scan your home network and use the pre-installed skills to locate devices. Whatever you've named them your app will be the default name when it's sucked into the Alexa app.

Rename your devices in the Alexa app

Alexa will take the name of a device, found in its native app – but this can lead to clashes between devices, if for example, you have two different manufacturers of smart bulb, which have both defaulted to "lounge light" for example. The result can be chaotic.

However, you can name devices in the Alexa app separately, so you'll want to go through and give them all easy-to-remember and logical names. Also, avoid clashes in Alexa between even random types of device. Having a "lounge" Sonos speaker and "lounge lamp" can play havoc with Alexa, so try and keep things separate.

To rename head to the Alexa app > Smart Home tab at the bottom. Choose the type of product from the screen, which makes it easier to find the exact device. Tap on a device, choose the menu and tap Edit name.

Set up Alexa groups

From within the Smart Home menu of the Amazon Alexa smartphone app, you can add any device into a single group, which can be controlled by voice.

It's pretty easy to do. Head to the Alexa app > Smart Home > press the + button in the top right > Add group. Choose Smart Home Group and give it a name that you'll remember. This could be "main lights" or "downstairs lights" for example. Tap the devices you want from within the list, and then you're done.

Import scenes from third party apps

If you've designed scenes within apps such as Philips Hue, Alexa will also detect and import them. During a scan of your network, scenes will be added to the Alexa app. You just need to have installed the relevant skills. Once registered in the app, you can then ask Alexa to control them.

What Alexa commands can I use?

So you have your lights, cameras, plugs and more set up with Alexa, and your scenes and groups, too. Here's some ideas to get you started.

"Alexa, lights on."

"Alexa, lights off."

"Alexa, dim main lights to 50%."

"Set the light to blue."

"Set the light to soft white."

"Make the light warmer/cooler."

"Alexa, set the temperature to 21."

"Alexa, it's Bedtime" [to activate a Scene].

What happens if Alexa can't find your device?

If you've gone through all these steps and Alexa isn't seeing your device, there's some steps you can take. For brevity, here's your essential Alexa troubleshooting checklist

- Check it's a Works with Alexa product
- Is it powered on and ready to be discovered?
- Delete and reinstall the Alexa skill, and sign in
- Check your phone, Alexa and this device are all connected to the same Wi-Fi network

- Turn Alexa off, the device and check how to do a hardware reset

- Update your router settings

Creating an Amazon Household

The Amazon Echo Show is a fantastic tool for using your voice to manage everything from a shopping list to music playlist and to videos, but what if there are other people in your household? For people with multi-person households, especially where members of that household all have purchased various content on Amazon like music and audiobooks, then it makes a lot of sense to enabled shared profiles so that you can listen to each other's music. In addition to sharing music, you can also share shopping lists, to-dos, calendar entries, and other features available on the Echo/Alexa system.

Let's us look at how you can add a profile to your Amazon Echo Show. All these actions can be performed by visiting echo.amazon.com, or through the Alexa App on your smart device. To add someone using the App, go to the menu sidebar and select **Settings**, under Settings select **Accounts** and choose **Household profiles,** you will then need to follow the on-screen instructions. Also, know that the person you desire to add may needs to be present to input their credentials.

Another method is to go to amazon.com and select **Accounts & Lists** near the top of the page, then select "Your Account." Go to the bottom right and select **shopping programs and rentals,** then select **Amazon Households.** Then select your desired option, **add adult**, **add** a **teen** and **add a child,** to follow the instructions.

Alexa App Home Page

You can view the App layout at alexa.amazon .com. Basically, the menu of app pages is on the left and the current page will be on the right. Also, you can see this display in large mobile devices, but the three horizontal lines which is depicted as the Menu, and the current page is what is normally displayed on most phones and tablets. At the top of the Home page, it will display **things to try**, **your cards** and the recent **music player**.

Things to try: this feature appears at the top of the Alexa App Home page. It rotates through some suggestions about 7-9 seconds of things you can say to Alexa, and these suggestions are mostly the trending or current issues. Below the suggestions there are shaded buttons, I normally tap through them to see the suggestions since I don't have the patience to wait for them rotate. There are few times I find things of interest at the suggestion, but when I don't see any, I focus on more important things than wasting time.

Player: When you load your media either playing or paused, you will see a player at the bottom of the app Home page. This allows you to control it, and you will see in the bar an icon of the current song in the queue. What I love about the player feature is that any page you are on, it will always display at the bottom of the App.

Cards: you create a card base on the frequent verbal interaction with Alexa. The primarily purpose of the card is to preserves the request and response from Alexa such as music station, videos, or forecast requested, and some items you added to your shopping list. All these things mentioned and other most verbal interactions form your card and the card forms your Alexa Dialog History. You scroll down to access the card or go through **settings** and select **history**.

Card options: you will see the top card in your history with several options:

- **Remove card:** This option is used to delete the card

- **Give voice feedback:** This feature is use to access the questions or commands you gave to Alexa and the feedback received. You will be able to know if Alexa is giving you the right answer or not, and you can give your feedback with "Yes" or "No." However, if you are unsatisfied with Alexa response, kindly answer "No" and an option to send more detailed feedback to Amazon will be given to you. If Alexa is not carrying out your instruction, you can can do a voice training by going to **Settings>Accounts> Voice Training**

- **Learn More:** The learn more option will take you to Alexa, and Alexa Device FAQs, which serves as another crucial part of the Help & Feedback section Menu. I will advice you check them out when you are less busy.

Note: you can only delete your entire history by deregistering your device. I sometimes use this feature when I want to give away my device as a gift or sell it out. However, you can choose to deregister and reregister your device. Check the settings section to see more explanation.

- **Wikipedia & Bing Search:** one or both of these search engine options might appear on a card. There are times the Card displayed a short answer and the link to the subject on Wikipedia, but this depends on the topic you asked Alexa about. Also, Alexa might be unclear about what you asked and it will give you the option to search Bing for that person, place, thing or whatever your query was about. The only search engine option on the app is Bing.

Playing Audiobooks With The Echo Show

This is a unique feature that enables you to listen to vast library of written materials. Audible is an Amazon company with a significant improvement from just audiobooks to podcast for over the few years. There are so many benefits of having audible account. Let us look at few of them:

- You have a 30-day free audible trial
- Free audible app that allows you to listen on your devices
- Over 180,000 thousands titles at your selection
- You get 30% discount on additional books
- You have an exchange period to trade a book for

another that you don't like

- o You get all those benefits with a monthly fee of $14.95, with the option to opt out at any time.

If you are interested to sign up for audible account, visit audible.com and sign in into your Amazon account, choose existing payment method or add new payment method, select your membership, then select your free book. You can enjoy the free 30 days trial but make sure you cancel within the 30 days to avoid being charged.

Integrating Echo Show with Audible

After registering for audible account, it is time to connect Alexa with Audible. All you need to do is to visit the Alexa App and select **music, video & books**, scroll down to the bottom and select **audible** from the books section, select **link account** and follow the prompts. However, if you had an audible account where you have purchased audible books, you will see the book in the audible section of the App.

Now that you have your Audible books ready, it is time to enjoy it on Echo Show. Just choose any title you want to hear either using voice or manual control. I normally use the voice control because Alexa is very good at carrying out instructions in this area. Simply say to Alexa, "Read my Audible book" and Alexa will normally ask you which book, make sure you request by title. Don't forget that you can also use the voice control to say things like resume, pause, go back, go forward etc.

How to listen to Kindle Books with the Echo Show

Since the introduction of Amazon's Kindle, it has been a dynamic eBook reader with awesome features for those who love eBooks. Now, you can use Echo Show to listen to Kindle Books. Amazing! You can either purchased a kindle book individually or be a member of Kindle Unlimited with a monthly fee of $99.9, and you will have unlimited reading of over 1 million book titles. You can find out the benefits of this offer on Amazon site.

Integrating Echo Show with Kindle

The process remains the same. Simply go to the Alexa App and select Music, Video & Books, and then scroll down to the books section to select Kindle, link your account when requested. Choose any Kindle book and it will show on the list.

After integrating Alexa with Kindle, you can now enjoy your kindle audiobooks on your Echo Show by simply going to the kindle section and select the title you want to hear or make use of your voice to place the request, and you will see the book shows up on the device and the Alexa App player. You can then use the voice control to navigate through the book. Echo Show is indeed an amazing device!

How to Use Echo Show to Make a Call & send a Message

The Echo Show device can be used to make a call or send a message but the individual you intended calling or messaging must have a compatible device such as a smartphone, tablet or Echo and must have installed the Alexa App. However, for you to use the video call feature, the person you want to call must also have the Echo Show device or preferably a video enable phone that has the Alexa App installed. Please, be aware that it is only those in your contact list that you can call.

If you want to make a video call, all you need to do is to tap on the onscreen icon for video call and Alexa will connect you, or you use the option of calling the person's name. For example, say, "Call aunt Gretchen," and Alexa will begin the call. **Note**: on the Echo Show, if you are calling a person that has the Echo Show device, the default call made will be a video. But you can command Alexa to turn off the video by simply saying, "Turn video off," or select the video icon on the touch screen.

You can also make a call from the Alexa App by selecting the Conversations icon, select the New Conversation icon, and choose a contact and the phone icon for a video call. Also, if you have a call from someone, Alexa will notify you and display the contact on the screen, and you will see the green light appear on your device. You can answer the call by selecting the Answer button on the device screen or by saying, "Answer." You can also end the call by using the End-call button on the screen or simply tell Alexa, "Hang up." To ignore the call, do the same by saying to her, "Ignore the call."

If you want to use Alexa for messaging, you have to understand that messages are recorded and played back to the recipient rather than transcribed and read by Alexa. You can send a message by using the App, select the Conversations icon > New Conversation icon, and choose a contact before following the prompts, or use the keyboard icon and type a message, then use the Send button. Another way you can send a message is by saying, "Send a message to Jennifer Lopez," and Alexa will prompt you for the message and send the message after completion.

You can reply a message from the App, all you need to do is to select the conversation from those shown, press the Microphone icon and speak your message, release the Mic when you are done to send the message or slide to left to cancel the message. When you see a yellow light bar of Echo Show that is a notification that you have one or more messages waiting. You can hear the messages by saying to Alexa, "Play my messages." But if you have more than one number that is synced with Alexa, name the number by saying, "Play messages for _____" to hear only your messages.

Weather And Other Location

You can use the Echo Show to Access the weather, just tell Alexa, "Show me the weather," the screen will show the weather information of your location. If you want to see the weather of another location, provide Alexa with the location. You can also request from Alexa the next day weather or any other time or day, if the information is available, the device will display it.

It is also possible to customize the weather information to show temperature in Fahrenheit or Celsius.

Location

During the setup process of the Echo Show, your time zone, locations, and other locality features were automatically records. If you wish to change your location and the features, simply say, "Alexa, go to settings," you can then select settings>device options>device location, you can then use the keyboard to enter your new location.

Find Local Businesses And Restaurants Including Reviews

Now that I have thought you how to set your location, Alexa will know the exact place to search when you ask questions about businesses and restaurants. When you asked Alexa about business, about three information will be displayed on the screen, the name of the business, a brief description and the distance from your location. You can view more details by sliding the screen to the left. You can ask Alexa, "What supermarkets are nearby?" "Find an African restaurant, or is the post office open?" also, you can ask Alexa some information when planning a trip. For instance "Is there a shoe store in New York?' Whatever searches you made, Cards are produced, that puts the result on the Alexa App

I believe you have started seeing the amazing benefits of this device. you can search for traffic information, movies, hear the news, sports such as Major League Baseball, National Football League, National Hockey League, Women's National Basketball Association, Major League, Soccer, UEFA Champions League, English Premier League and host of others.

Other Devices:

Set Up Do Not Disturb

The Echo Show has Skills, messages, and calls notifications that can sometimes be distracting, so the

Do Not Disturb (DND) feature becomes very handy. This feature keeps Echo Show quiet including preventing incoming calls. To activate the option, simply swipe down from top to the bottom of the screen and you will see the DND button that you can turn on or off. You can also go to the menu and select **settings>Do Not Disturb** feature.

Turn Off The Screen

Sometimes, you don't want other persons to know what you are doing on your Echo Show, all you need to do is to issue a command to Alexa by saying "Alexa, turn off the screen," and the screen will go off. You can also use the wake word to turn it on or touch the screen. To put off the device completely, press down the mute button for some seconds.

Voice Training

Alexa has a good voice recognition technology, but when she begins to misunderstand you when you make requests, then voice training might be the needful. Simply go to **settings > voice training > next** to start the session. There are 25 phrases of the most common syllable used in English that you can say so that Alexa will learn the way you say them. Every time you select voice training, you will always get a different request list, if you don't want to go through the entire list, you can return and you will get new requests to repeat when you try it again.

Sports Update

This is one good feature that allows you to follow professional leagues and teams from Europe and North America including basketball and football for most of the major colleges in the United States. If you want to follow any team, use the Search your Teams box to select a particular team of your choice. Once you click on those teams from the search result, they will appear in your list.

Calendars

Alexa has the capacity to link to calendars from Google, Apple icloud, and Microsoft. You can link your calendars and add items to them with basic requests such as "Add appointment at 1pm Monday to my calendar," and a lot of other similar things. To use this feature, go to Settings, select Account and scroll down to Calendars. Select the calendar you plan to connect, and select Link ___ account. If you want to see what is in your calendar, say, "What's on my calendar or Show me my calendar."

Create multiple profiles

Alexa will listen to anyone – but that doesn't mean she has to treat everyone the same. If you set up separate profiles for each person in your household, you can switch between them to ensure that any music played, calendars accessed, and accounts used for shopping will be appropriate to that particular user.

Creating a new profile has to be done by the registered owner of the Echo device. Open Settings in the Alexa app, click Household Profile in the Settings section and then enter your account password. Now get the other member to log in using the same device and link your accounts.

A word of warning: when you tell Alexa to order an item from Amazon, the system will use whichever payment method is set up for the active profile – so to avoid mix-ups, it's worth checking before you place the order. To do so, just ask "Alexa, which profile is this?"

Protect your purchases

On the subject of voice purchases, if you've got kids in the house you'll probably want to set up a PIN code for online shopping, to ensure they don't order a new LEGO kit every two weeks. To do this, scroll down to Voice Purchasing in the Alexa app and add the code in the "Require voice code" field. This will need to be spoken when making a purchase – so make sure they don't overhear you.

Use IFTTT

You probably already know about the free-to-use automation service IFTTT – the web service is now used by supermarkets among other parties. For home use, though, what's perhaps more handy is the numerous Alexa integrations the service now offers.

To get started, go to ifttt.com/amazon_alexa and click Connect. Enter your password on the Amazon page that appears and authorise the connection. You can now use the pre-rolled applets to link Alexa to a huge range of services and devices – from a Roomba vacuum cleaner or a WeMo coffee maker to Facebook Messenger and Google spreadsheets.

In our view, one of the most useful integrations is between Alexa and task management app Wunderlist: although Alexa already has a native shopping-list feature, Wunderlist is more flexible and works across almost every platform imaginable.

To set it up, search IFTTT for "wunderlist" and you should see a result entitled "Add Amazon Echo shopping list items to Wunderlist". Click the Turn On toggle switch, and on the next screen enter "me@wunderlist.com" in the "To:" field, before clicking Save.

Now open IFTTT's settings (by clicking your name at the top of the IFTTT interface) and link your Google account. If you have more than one Google account, make a note of the one you used.

Finally, sign in to Wunderlist and open your account settings, again by clicking your name at the top of the sidebar. Click "Add or manage your email addresses", and make sure that the email address you just linked to IFTTT is allowed to add items to your list by email. Now, when you tell Alexa to add something to your shopping list, it will be forwarded onto Wunderlist, ready for you to pick up on the web or on your phone.

Personalise your Flash Briefing

A Flash Briefing is Amazon's name for a quick info dump that draws content from multiple sources, such as news publishers, weather forecasters and exchange rate trackers. To set one up that's personalised just for you, open the Alexa app and click Flash Briefing in the Settings section. Click "Get more Flash Briefing content" and select the elements you would like to add: you will find options such as BBC World Service, The Guardian, MTV and the Joke of the Day.

Each one you add will be automatically enabled, but you can remove any source from the briefing if you choose: just return to the Flash Briefing section and toggle the switch beside each one's name.

You can enable sports content within the Flash Briefing, too – but Alexa already knows a lot about football and other sports. Click Sports Update on the Settings screen, then use the search box to find the teams you're interested in. As well as the huge Premier League clubs, you will also find local teams such as

Leatherhead and Taunton Town – although, tragically, Lewes FC is missing from the list.

Say goodbye, Alexa

If you're upgrading from a Dot to a Plus, or from a regular Alexa to a Show, you might be tempted to pass your old device on to a friend, or sell it online. Before you do, make sure you deregister it so that the new owner can't place online orders using your account. Open the Alexa app, click Settings, then click on the name of the device you're getting rid of. You will find the deregistration option in the About section.

Don't worry about the record that Alexa keeps of things you've said to her: this won't follow the device to its new home. However, if you ever want to purge this information from your own account, you can delete individual recordings from the homepage of the Alexa app, or switch to your Amazon account to delete the lot.

To do this, log in at amazon.co.com, click Your Account, and find the link to "Manage Your Content and Devices". Switch to the Your Devices tab, click the three dots beside the names of each of your Echo speakers, and choose "Manage voice recordings" on each one. Read the disclaimer and click Delete to wipe the slate clean.

Top essential Alexa Skills to try first

Having tried and tested some of the most popular Alexa skills, here are the ones you'll want to get right away, a handful of niceties worth checking out, and some you'll want to avoid for now.

1. Roomba: Control your robot vac

iRobot's Roomba robot vacs are some of the best around, and now they'll digest your voice commands as well as gobbling up stray pet hairs.

Well, if you have one of the fancier web connected Roomba models, such as the 900 Series – and live in the US – that is.

The latest major update to the iRobot HOME App for Android and iOS introduces the skill, so all you need to do is say, "Alexa, tell Roomba to start cleaning," and you can kick back with your beverage of choice.

It's frustrating that it's currently limited to the States, of course, but no one said living the smart home dream was going to be easy.

2. Skill Finder: Find more skills!

Amazon has introduced a neat Alexa skill that will helps you find more Alexa skills.

It's a quick and easy way to discover cool new integrations you might not know about, simply by asking things like, "Alexa, tell Skill Finder to give me the Skill of the Day".

Alternatively, it'll let you unearth skills on a category-by-category basis, so query, "Alexa, tell Skill Finder to list the top skills in the games category," and you'll be served up the most popular gaming-related integrations.

3. Plex: Manage your media

This is probably our new favourite Alexa skill as it lets you control your media library without lifting a finger.

If you use Plex Media Server and have an Echo device in your living room, you can now ask Alexa to play films, tell you what's next on your Plex deck, and even suggest things you might want to want.

"Alexa, play the next episode of Prison Break but don't tell my boss!"

4. TrackR: Find your phone

If you sign up for a TrackR account, you can shout 'Alexa, find my phone' and your handset will immediately ring at full volume. It's properly useful for forgetful people and works a treat.

5. Hive: Control your heating

The Hive skill lets you control the temperature of your house using Alexa – and there's a bit of banter for good measure.

If you turn the heating off when your house is warm, Alexa might comment; and by comment, we mean she'll say something that comes off as slightly sarcastic.

Still, it saves you the effort of actually having to get up to adjust the temperature.

6. Hue: Control your lights

Your Echo assistant has known how to play nice with Hue lights for a while, but these days you have more mood control options than ever.

Want to make things all sexy? Set up a 'romantic' profile and Alexa will make your bedroom redder than downtown Amsterdam before you can so much as say, "Giggity."

7. Control your thermostat

Alexa now supports the Nest range of Learning Thermostats, meaning you can simply say "Hey Alexa, raise the living room temperature by 2 degrees," and you'll be toastier than chestnuts roasting on an open fire.

8. Uber: Call for a ride

Uber is a little fiddly to set up with Alexa, but once you've got it sorted, it does feel a little bit like magic.

It took us a couple of attempts to link an Uber account to our Echo, and If you try to just ask for an Uber,   Alexa will tell you to ask for it in a specific way.

After you've got the knack though, just say the necessary incantation and a ride will roll up outside your location. Neat.

9. 7-Minute Workout: Get a guide workout

Just say, "Alexa, start 7-minute workout," and shock of all horrors, Alexa will take your candy ass through a 7-minute workout!

If you're unsure of any of the exercises, the app on your phone will show you little pictures of what you should do.

It'd be nice if Alexa was a bit more encouraging, or played some music to help motivate you, but it's pretty good all the same.

10. Spotify: The best for music streaming

Spotify is the best music streaming service around, and with Echo, Premium subscribers can simply shout out what they want to be played, be it a specific artist, mood, playlist and even decade.

It's a no-brainer to enable as soon as you fire up your new smart speaker and, better still, it comes pre-loaded – just enable it as your default music player and you're away.

11. Wake up to your favourite song

While we're on the subject of music, as of December 18, Echo users can now command Alexa to wake them up to the tunes of their choice. Whether you need some heavy metal to stun you out of your slumber, or some Marvin Gaye for a relaxing Sunday morning in bed with the paper, Alexa has you covered.

You won't need an additional Skill download for this; just say "Alexa wake me at 8am to…" and choose from artists, playlists, tracks or even a random selection. Best news is it works with all supported music services.

12. Control your whole home entertainment set-up

If you're the proud owner of a Logitech Harmony Hub and a compatible remote, then you can use your Echo to add voice controls. You can command Alexa to turn on the TV or media player, or play and pause content on your television screen, This is particularly handy if you've lost the remote down the back of the sofa.

A recent improvement even simplified the voice controls. You can simply say "Alexa, turn up the volume/turn on BBC 1."

13. The Guardian: All the latest news

Ask Alexa for the latest news, headlines, podcasts and more with this skill – she'll even read your entire articles if you want.

It's well useful for all those times you want to meditate on how horrible the world is whilst doing the washing up.

14. Sky Sports: Never miss a goal

Getting mad when your team concedes a last minute equalizer has never been easier, as Alexa will feed you back all the latest scores and sport news.

It's available on your snazzzy right out of the box, so all you have to do is ask.

15. National Rail: Get train updates

Gone are the days of having to fiddle with an app to find out Southern's fecked up your commute again.

With Echo, all you'll need to do is chat to Alexa for a breakdown of the latest morning misery. Crying into your porridge? That bit will likely remain a constant.

16. Google Calendar: Never miss a meeting again

Habitually late to – or forget – pretty much everything? Alexa might just be your saviour, as you can ask your Echo to remind you about meetings and other important events

Neglected an anniversary, for example? Combine your reminder with begging Alexa to order some last minute flowers for the ultimate in time-efficient getting out of jail.

17. Control Fire TV with your Echo

Most Amazon Fire TV devices now come with an Alexa voice remote, but if it's across the other side of the room, that's a whole lot of energy expenditure that could be used for keeping warm. So, US Echo owners (and we're hoping UK soon), can now control their Fire TV devices with Alexa on the Amazon Echo.

You could say "Alexa open Hulu" or Alexa "show me comedy films" for example. You can even say "Show me films with Clint Eastwood," leveraging the universal search feature.

If you only have one Fire TV, Alexa should complete the pairing process automatically.

How to set up and use Alexa smart home groups

One of the main problems with a house stuffed full of smart home kit is having to try and remember what you've called everything: was it the lounge light or the living room light that you wanted to turn on? Now, with Alexa's improved smart home groups, that pain goes away. I'll show you how to set up and use Alexa smart home groups.

Groups have been available for a while but Amazon has dramatically improved them. Now, you can group your Echo devices with your smart home devices, which tells Alexa where it's located. That makes control far easier. For example, once you've grouped items together, you can just say, "Alexa, turn on the light", and your Echo understands which light your talking about with no further clarification. And, an update to the Sonos skill means that when you now talk to Alexa, on the Sonos player in the same room ducks its volume rather than your entire system.

Groups make it easier to understand and manage your home, too, as you place everything in one room together. In short, if you've got more than one Echo device, you'll want to follow these instructions. Please note, that not all third-party Amazon Alexa devices can be put into groups. For example, if you buy the Netgear Orbi Voice, it won't let you place it in a group. Using third-party devices often means going back to the older form of control where you tell Alexa which device you want to control.

1. Create a smart home group

Open the Alexa app and tap the Devices icon at the bottom-right of the screen. This will take you to the main smart home screen, listing all of your devices plus any groups that you might have. To add a new group tap the Plus icon and select Add group. You'll be given a list of common room names that you can choose from, although you can type in a custom name if you prefer. Tap Next when you're done.

Next, on the Define Group page you'll be given a list of smart devices that you can add. Choose the devices that are in this room, including any Amazon Echo devices, Sonos speakers, smart lights and even thermostats. Don't worry if you miss anything, as you can edit a Group later and add or remove devices. Tap Save when you're done.

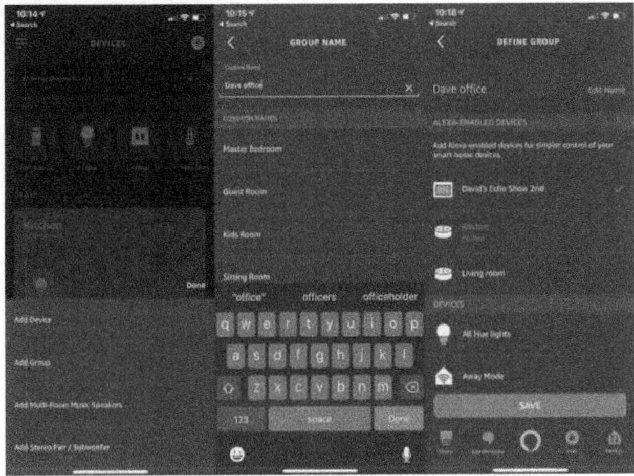

2. Control your devices with the app

Back on the Devices page, you'll see your new group. Tap a group and you'll see all of your devices in there; you can tap Edit to make changes to the devices.

At the top of a group's page are All On and All Off buttons. Tap these to turn your group devices on or off. Note that this feature only works on devices that have switch-like capabilities, such as smart plugs and smart lights.

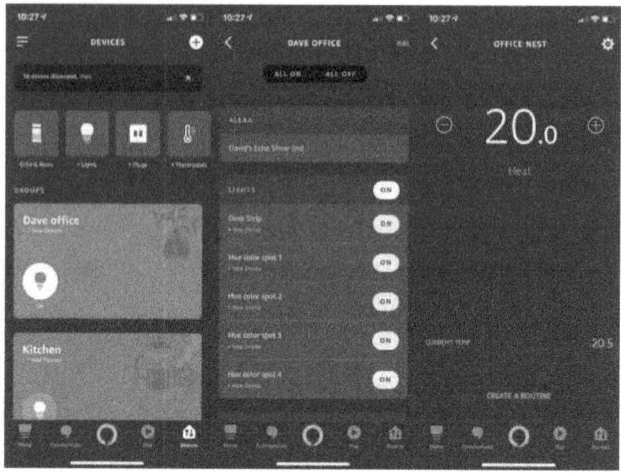

3. Control your devices with your voice

When you talk to an Echo that's in a group, you can use simplified commands to control smart devices. Here are a few to get you started:

"Alexa, turn on lights."

"Alexa, turn off lights."

"Alexa, set temperature to 19 degrees."

"Alexa, what is the thermostat temperature?"

This type of command is far easier than remembering device or group names. To control other devices from your grouped Echo, you can use the old style of command, naming the smart home device that you want to control, such as "Alexa, turn on office light."

4. Edit Alexa smart home device groups

Once you have created an Alexa smart home group you can change its settings and rename it. To do this just go to the Smart Home menu in the Alexa app, select Groups and choose the group you want to edit.

You can change the group name by selecting Edit Name, add or remove devices from the group or delete the group entirely by hitting the trash icon.

How to make Alexa Routines – smart home automation made easy

One of the best updates to the Echo family is Alexa Routines, enabling you to control multiple devices and perform multiple actions via a single phrase, such as "Alexa, goodbye". No longer do you have to reel off a long list of instructions – through simple automation, you can control devices faster.

Whether you want to turn off everything as you leave your home, or set your home up perfectly for a movie night, we'll show you how to build your own Routines. Since Alexa works in the cloud, these instructions apply for all devices, including the Echo, Echo Spot, Echo Show and Echo Dot.

Before you start, you'll need to have added any smart home devices that you want to control to your Amazon Alexa account.

1. Create a new Routine

Launch the Amazon Alexa app on your phone, tap the hamburger and select Routines. You'll see that there's a pre-made "Alexa, start my day" routine in there; we'll skip this for now, so tap the Create Routine button.

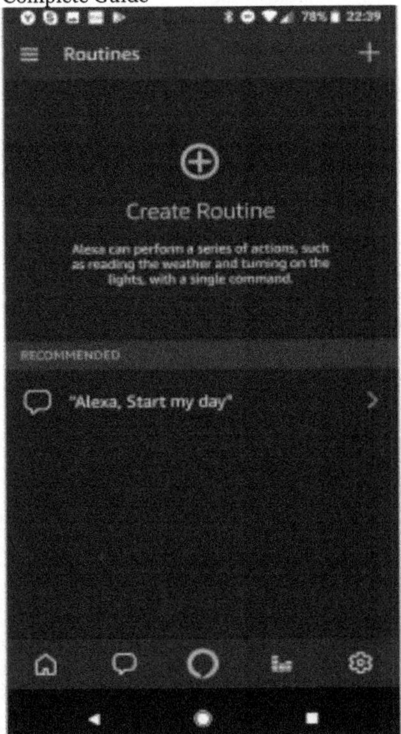

2. Create the start action

Routines can be triggered by a phrase, or set to turn on at a specific time (repeat options for multiple days are available). We'll start with a phrase, so tap "When you say something". Enter the word or phrase that you want to use: I've gone for "Alexa, Goodbye", so I can trigger the routine when I go out. Tap Save when you're done.

3. Choose your smart home actions

Tap Add action, then choose Smart Home. You can now choose to Control device or Control scene. Scenes are discovered by Alexa for certain products, such as a specific Philips Hue lighting mode.

Select Control device, and you'll see a list of your smart home devices. Currently, Alexa Routines can only control devices that have an on/off mode, or a brightness slider. This means you can't control a thermostat's temperature, for example.

Exact control differs from device to device. For example, with the Honeywell Evohome smart heating system, you can trigger modes such as Away, which sets every zone to 15ºC by default.

When selected most devices give you the option to turn them on or off; smart lighting options give you a brightness slider if you select to turn them off.

Select the option you want for the device you've selected and tap Next, and then tap Add. Repeat this step for any other smart home devices you want to control.

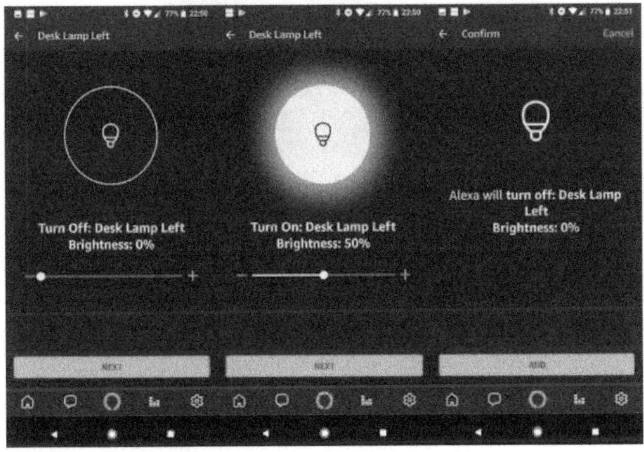

4. Choose other actions

As well as controlling smart home devices, Routines can also do other things: News reads out your Flash Briefing; Traffic gives you an update between the addresses set in your Alexa account; Weather gives you a local weather update; and Alexa Says lets you choose what Alexa will say when the Routine runs, choosing from a list of canned responses. Add as many other actions as you want.

5. Select the responding device

If you choose any option that requires Alexa to speak, such as a weather report, you can use the From option to pick which device will be used for the audio. You can force Alexa to speak from a set Echo, but the default option of "The device you speak to" is probably best, so Alexa will respond from which ever Echo you activated.

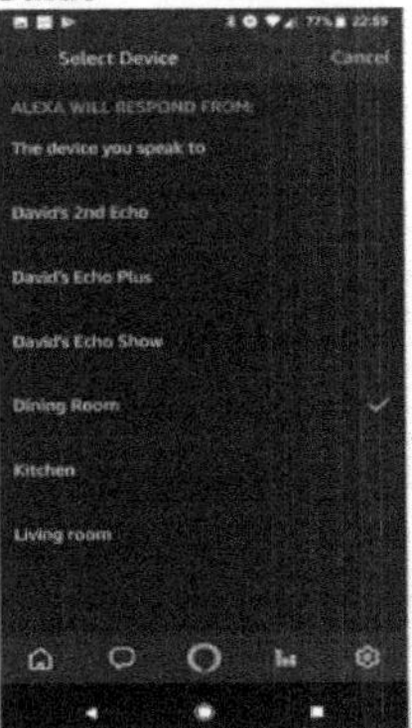

6. Create and run your routine

Tap the Create button and your Routine will be created. As the message says, it can take up to one minute for routines to be created and available. If you picked a time-based trigger, your routine will be activated automatically. Otherwise, you can just say your phrase, such as "Alexa, goodbye".

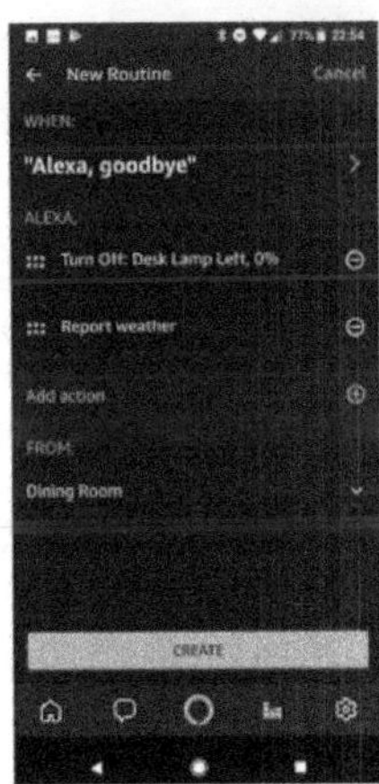

How to make Skype calls with Amazon Alexa

Amazon Echo devices already let you make voice and video calls between each other for free. As of a more recent update, you can now extend the capability and make Skype calls, too.

As well as making standard VoIP calls, you can use Skype to call landline numbers, and you get 200 free minutes to use. This puts Alexa closer to Google Assistant, which already gives you free landline calls. Incoming calls can also be answered from your Echo devices.

Getting it all working requires a bit of configuration, but we'll take you through the exact steps here.

Step 1 – Add the Skype Skill

Fire up the Amazon Alexa app and tap the menu button. Select Settings and tap Communications. Currently, there's only one option: Skype. Tap the Plus icon next to Skype and choose Sign In. You'll be redirected to a sign-in page, so just enter your Skype username and password when prompted.

Once signed in, you'll get a page showing all the things that Alexa will be able to do with your Skype account. Tap Yes to continue.

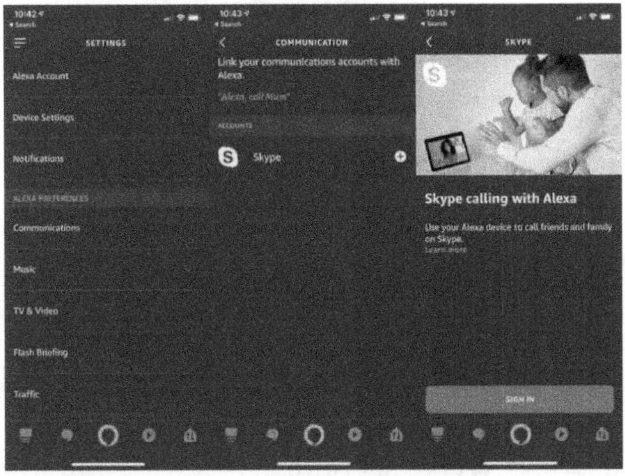

Step 2 – Confirm your settings

Once complete, you'll get a message telling you that your Skype is linked. Tap Done to confirm the changes. You'll then see the screen that shows you that your Skype account is linked to Alexa. If you change your mind, you can tap the Unlink account button.

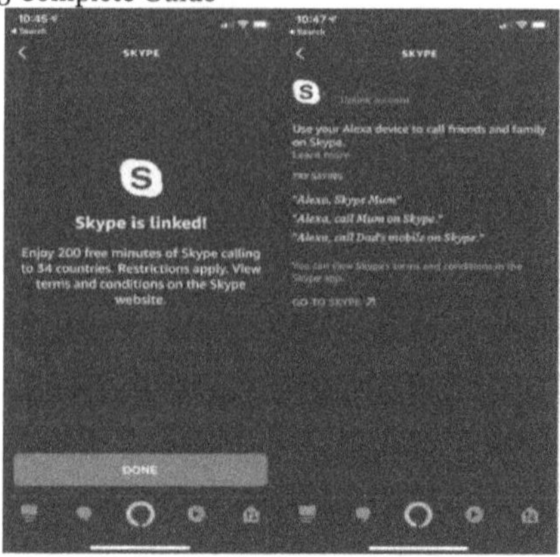

Step 3 – Make a call

Just say, "Alexa, Skype <name of contact>" and the call will be made. The Skype skill will pull contacts from your Skype account; if you install the mobile version, you can synchronise the contacts from your phone with your account to make things easy.

If you want to call a number that's not in your address book, you can just ask Alexa to call it (say the actual number) instead. Please note that the Skill can't look up local business addresses, which is a limitation compared to the Google Assistant skill.

All calls made go out without a Caller ID. If you have a Skype phone number, then calls are made with this.

You can't synchronise your phone's Caller ID as you can with Google Home calling, though.

Step 4 – Answer a call

Incoming Skype calls will ring your Echo devices. To answer, just say, "Alexa, pick up". You'll then be connected to your call. You can say, "Alexa, hang up" to put down any call.

Amazon Alexa – Drop in, calls and messages

Amazon recently added voice and video calls, and the drop-in intercom feature. Both work either locally inside your home, or externally to friends with Echo devices who are in your contacts book. The difference between a call and drop-in is how the person at the other end responds.

A call has to be answered, making it useful for talking to a friend over the internet; all of their Echo devices will ring (bar those set to Do Not Disturb).

Drop-ins are automatically connected, making the Echo a useful intercom system for the home, or just to see what's going on at home when you're out. Drop-in settings are managed by device. By default, drop-in is only enabled for members of your household and contacts with permission, but you can change that to only household members, or disable the feature entirely.

Amazon also has Announcements, where you can transmit a voice message to all Echo devices in your home ("Alexa, announce dinner is ready"). If you want to get the kids' attention, then it's a handy tool and matches Google Home's Broadcast feature.

Call quality, both audio and video, is excellent. I find it particularly useful in-house as a way to talk to other people when I'm too lazy to stand up and move. A recent update lets you make calls or drop in from the Alexa app on your phone or tablet, too.

With the Skype integration, you can hook your Alexa speakers up to your VoIP account and make calls. These can either be over the internet (Skype-to-Skype) or telephone calls using your Skype credit. That's not quite as powerful as the free landline and mobile calls that Google gives you with the Google Home.

You also can't set the outbound caller ID to match that of your mobile phone, as you can with Google. The nearest option is to buy a number from Skype and make out-bound calls from this. Alexa can call anyone in your Skype address book, although you can manually say a number to call, too. It's a shame that you can't just say the name of local business.

151

CPSIA information can be obtained
at www.ICGtesting.com
Printed in the USA
LVHW100236291122
734233LV00003B/890